# a *Special* SEASON

## Players' Reflections on an Inspiring Year

Mike Matheny·Matt Morris·Jason Isringhausen·Fernando Viña
Andy Benes·Kerry Robinson·Miguel Cairo

### By Rob Rains

SP

SPORTS
PUBLISHING
L.L.C.

www.SportsPublishingLLC.com

© 2003 Rob Rains
All Rights Reserved

Director of production: Susan M. Moyer
Developmental editor: Erin Linden-Levy
Copy editor: Cindy McNew
Interior design: Tracy Gaudreau
Dust jacket design: Kenneth J. O'Brien

ISBN: 1-58261-657-4

Printed in the United States Of America

Sports Publishing L.L.C.
www.sportspublishingllc.com

DEDICATED TO THE MEMORIES OF
JACK BUCK AND DARRYL KILE.

# INTRODUCTION

The Cardinals have been playing baseball continuously in St. Louis since 1892. In their more than 100-year history, they have won world championships, they have won National League pennants, and they have enjoyed Hall of Fame performers and spectacular single-season performances.

But they never before experienced a season like 2002.

Perhaps no team in baseball has been as tested as the Cardinals were in 2002. Through it all, they displayed class and dignity and somehow still found a way to go out and play quality, winning baseball.

One week in June will be remembered forever not only by the players, management and staff of the Cardinals but by their fans in St. Louis, around the country and throughout the world.

Even though it was well known that legendary broadcaster Jack Buck was very ill, the news that he had died still gave the team and the city of St. Louis a tremendous shock.

Only days later, after mourning Buck's death, came another stunning jolt—pitcher Darryl Kile was found dead in his hotel room in Chicago.

This death was *not* understandable. At the age of 33, Kile was seemingly healthy and in the prime of his life. He had just been with his teammates a day earlier. He went to dinner, then to his hotel room to go to sleep and never woke up.

His death was a tremendous blow, not only because of his on-field contributions, but because Kile was one of the most popular players on the team. He was a leader in the clubhouse and he was a friend to everybody.

Kile's death affected everyone connected with the team—the front office, the media, the people who worked in the clubhouse. Their lives had all been touched by Kile, and all of a sudden he was gone.

Somehow, the Cardinals' players had to come to grips with their emotions enough to continue the fight that Kile had pursued—trying to win the division title, then the pennant, and finally the World Series.

A new battle cry seemed to rally the Cardinals—"For Darryl". They were still mourning his loss, but the players were strengthened by the knowledge that going out and winning games was the best tribute they could give to their fallen teammate.

Kile's last victory with the Cardinals—on the night Buck died—put the team into first place in the National League's Central Division. The team stayed there for the rest of the season.

On the day Kile died, the Cardinals had 40 victories. With their final win on the last day of the regular season, their total stood at 97 victories. After Kile's death, they won 57 games—matching his uniform number. A coincidence? Maybe, but maybe not.

There were amazing success stories during the season. Pitcher Jason Simontacchi, a 28-year-old rookie and a former tow truck driver who had pitched for Italy in the 2000 Olympics, was called up from the minors and won 11 games. Pitcher Andy Benes floundered at the start of the season, took two months off, and many people thought he had retired. Instead, he came back to post the lowest ERA in the NL over the second half of the season.

Albert Pujols showed he was more than just a rookie sensation, following up his Rookie of the Year season with an even better sophomore year, finishing as the runner-up to the Giants' Barry Bonds in the MVP voting. He became the first player in major-league history to hit 30 homers, drive in 100 runs, score more than 100 runs and hit .300 in his first two major-league seasons.

The late-season addition of third baseman Scott Rolen in a trade from the Phillies brought another Silver Slugger and Gold Glove performer to the Cardinals, and also another player who understood exactly how to play the game.

Maybe that was why the 2002 season was such *A Special Season* for the Cardinals. They overcame tragedy and other obstacles but never wavered in their dedication to the game and their quest for the ultimate goal.

In the end, they came up seven wins short, losing the NL Championship Series to the Giants and failing to reach, and win, the World Series. Every player involved, however, knew it would be a season they would always remember.

Seven of those players—Mike Matheny, Matt Morris, Andy Benes, Fernando Vina, Jason Isringhausen, Kerry Robinson, and Miguel Cairo—agreed to share their thoughts about this remarkable season. Their thoughts are presented here, in journal form, with entries spread out through the course of the season.

Part of the beauty of baseball, of course, is that the Cardinals' quest to win the World Series didn't end in 2002. They get another chance this year. They will have new obstacles and new challenges, but the goal remains the same—to make the 2003 season something special as well.

(Tom Gannam, AP/Wide World Photos)

*Our new teammate Tino Martinez waves to the crowd on Opening Day in Busch Stadium. Busch is like no other place on Opening Day; the fans are great and there is a powerful energy running through the stadium.*

—— MIKE MATHENY

*E*very team tries to make Opening Day a big deal, but it's hard to top what goes on here. You watch the guys on the other team as you ride into the stadium, and you can tell they think it is something special. Today was no different, as we prepared to play Colorado.

I found out a few days ago, while we were still in spring training, that I wasn't going to start. Tony [La Russa] called me over in the outfield before a game against the Mets and we had a long talk. He told me I wasn't going to start Opening Day and I wasn't going to catch Matt [Morris]. He told me the first week we would be going off and on, and it looked like Mike [DeFelice] and I would each catch three games out of the first six. I was disappointed. Who wouldn't be? Who wouldn't want to catch Matt Morris? Who wouldn't want to catch Opening Day? Who wouldn't want to catch every day? There were reasons; Tony does everything for a reason. The reason is always what he feels is going to give us the best chance to win. Whether I wanted to hear it or not, I've never felt like it was anything personal. It was always the decision he felt was going to give us the best chance, not just to win each game, but to win for the whole season. I have to look at it from that perspective and realize that's his decision to make.

It's not the first time something like that has happened. I've been released twice and had teams tell me they didn't want me at all. This is a team that I know I am a big part of, and I know regardless of what happened on Opening Day that throughout the season I am going to have something to offer. The media made a lot out of it, and some of the other players made me dwell on it probably more than I otherwise would have. I would much rather have played, but I have to look at it from the team perspective.

Everybody is excited about our chances for the season. We have basically the same nucleus of last year's team, and we finished strong and had an exciting playoff. The team that beat us won the whole thing, so I think that has given us a lot of confidence. Mark McGwire retired, but I think everybody in the clubhouse was prepared for that. We didn't think he was coming back. My locker was next to his, and I could see his frustration and how tough it was for him. He saw an opportunity to move on with his life, and everybody was happy for him. Walt

[Jocketty] went out and signed Tino Martinez to replace him. He is coming in highly regarded and will add a lot to our club. We all are looking forward to picking his brain about all of the success he had with the Yankees.

The other big addition to the club is Jason Isringhausen, the new closer. It had been the top priority in the winter, and he should be a guy who will come in and be the power closer that the team needs. Matt is coming off a 22-win season, and Darryl [Kile] got his shoulder cleaned up over the winter and we know he is going to be healthy and ready to go. I feel healthy and know I am ready when I get the chance.

I do the same thing whenever I don't play. I stay in the dugout for the first six innings and really get a feel for the game, because up until that point you really don't

(Tom Gannam, AP/Wide World Photos)

*After losing Mark McGwire to retirement, we were desperate for a great first baseman. Walt Jocketty (left) really outdid himself when he signed Tino Martinez. Martinez is a natural leader and he brings a lot of experience from the Yankees.*

need two catchers in the bullpen. I try to do what I can to encourage guys and help from the bench. I always play mental games with myself, how we're pitching guys, how we're getting guys out, so that when I do come into the game I'm going to be ready.

We played a good game, winning 10-2. Winning the opener is always a big thing, because it just puts everybody in a good frame of mind and ready for the next day.

*M. M.*

—————— JASON ISRINGHAUSEN

The best thing about Opening Day was being able to ride in on the cars. All my family and friends that I grew up with were at the game. I had heard a lot about how special Opening Day was in St. Louis, but I had never been there because I had always been playing. As a kid I didn't go to many Cardinals games.

It was a very impressive ceremony, and then we went out and beat the Rockies 10-2. I got into the game to pitch the ninth inning, and even though we had a big lead, I was still nervous. I've always been nervous when I come in to pitch. I got the first ball and gave it to my father.

*J. I.*

—— KERRY ROBINSON

*H*aving grown up in St. Louis, I remember watching Opening Day as a kid, and I always said my goal was one day to play at Busch Stadium as a Cardinal. To be on the field as a player for the Cardinals was a great experience. I took my camcorder and recorded everything so that I will never forget it. I had looked forward to riding in those cars for a long time.

I also wanted to make sure it was a memorable day for my family. I brought my parents, my wife and my kids to the game in a limo. I wanted to make it a big deal for them.

It was a day I will never forget.

*K. R.*

—— MATT MORRIS

*I* didn't realize it until somebody reminded me that today was the third anniversary of the surgery on my elbow. All I was thinking about was going out and pitching well enough for us to beat the Astros—which we did, 7-3.

Ever since the surgery, I have tried to move forward. Even when I was rehabbing, I wanted to leave that behind me and just get back out on the mound. I didn't dwell on it. Mentally it was a lot harder than it was physically. All I had to do physically was regain the strength and flexibility. But mentally, not being with the guys every day, that was what really killed me. The team would leave town on a road trip, and I was still at home, working out every day at the stadium.

Luckily for me the injury was to my elbow, and there is a much higher rate of success and coming back than there is for other injuries. A shoulder seems like a much more complicated joint. I watched Alan Benes, because he and I were side by side during our rehabs and he had a lot more work to do than I did. The elbow bends at one position and that's it really. I didn't dwell too much on not getting back because I didn't want those negative things to be part of my vocabulary. I was just trying to get through it day by day, although some days were harder than others.

Two years was a long time, but what the injury taught me was that anything you set your mind to is achievable. Once I was able to get a full season in, since then, knock on wood, there's never been any soreness and I've never really iced my elbow. That's allowed me to get past it and not think about it also.

I think all of the time I spent working out at Busch while I was rehabbing is part of the reason I have had so much success in the park. All of the clubhouse guys were great to me; they kept my locker there the whole time even when I was hurt, and I just feel really comfortable there. I know where everybody is, I go through the same routine every game and it's just fabulous. Add the awesome fans to the mix, and I really get pumped up every time I get the chance to pitch there. I've been here for six years, and it has really been great.

The season is just getting started, but it looks like we could have something special happening this year.

*M. M.*

———— JASON ISRINGHAUSEN

*I* know this season is going to be different, pitching in front of my family and friends every day. Usually it happens that when my friends came to watch me pitch, I don't do too well. I hope it isn't going to be like that for the whole year. I don't think tickets are going to be a problem. A couple of guys come all the time and I leave them tickets, but that's about it. My parents don't come to many games. They would rather stay home and watch it on TV, where they can get the whole effect, than sit in the stands where they really can't see that well.

Pitching in St. Louis isn't going to add any extra pressure. I put enough pressure on myself as it is. Basically, I am a nervous

(James A. Finley, AP/Wide World Photos)

We all celebrate Eli Marrero's two-out, game-winning, bases-loaded single that scored J.D. Drew and gave Jason Isringhausen the win on April 13. We beat the Astros 2-1 at Busch Stadium.

wreck. We beat Houston 2-1 tonight and I got the win by striking out the side on nine pitches in the ninth. I didn't even realize I had done that until somebody was telling me it was some kind of record or something after the game. Things like that don't really click until later for me. Maybe later in my life it will mean more to me, but right now it was just a game and I am glad we won.

That's what I was supposed to do, and what I try to do every time I go into a game. I hadn't ever done that before, although once in the minors I did strike out four batters in an inning because of a passed ball or something.

It was nice to beat the Astros, because all of us pretty much believe Houston is the team we will have to beat to win the division.

*J. J.*

## APRIL 16, PHOENIX

—— ANDY BENES

*I* had a difficult time sleeping last night. I made my third start of the season, and the results were not good. My first start had been average and the second not very good. Then I went out against the Diamond-backs and gave up six hits and 10 runs in only three innings. Only three of the runs were earned because of errors, but I still knew I had not pitched very well. I take the way I do on the field very personally. I tend to carry it on my sleeve.

When I came back to the clubhouse before the game tonight, after finishing my pregame work, Walt Jocketty, our general manager, was in Tony's office. He said they needed to talk to me. Walt started out by saying that this was not one of his favorite conversations. I'm not very smart, but I knew the news was not going to be good. He said they needed to make a move and why didn't I think about it and let them know what I wanted to do.

There really were three choices—they could release me, they could disable me because of my knee, or I could retire. I think most people, if they have the choice of retiring or being fired, will take the option of saying they will retire because of personal pride. Nobody wants to be fired. Initially that was my thought, but I really had not thought about the big differences, legally and financially, that there are between the two. I did tell some of my teammates that it looked like this was it.

I was kind of surprised that it had all happened so quickly, because I really thought it was just a matter of locating my pitches. I had pitched well in spring training, but had been very disappointed in the starts in the regular season. I knew it wasn't going to be an option to continue to pitch in St. Louis, and I really wasn't that interested in going anywhere else to play.

I came back to St. Louis, thinking that maybe I had pitched my last game.

*A. B.*

——— MIKE MATHENY

*T*oday was an off day, and we were very happy for it. We lost to Milwaukee yesterday, as the Brewers completed a sweep of our four-game series. Any time you get swept you really want to get away and have a day to not think about baseball.

Our public relations director, Brian Bartow, and our traveling secretary, C. J. Cherre, contacted the Mets before we got to town and got the phone number of a person to give us a tour of the site of the terrorist attacks on the World Trade Center. A lot of the wives, players, coaches and Tony went down there on our bus. It was a gloomy day. We were given a unique opportunity to have an escort from the New York Police Department, and we went into some buildings across the street from the destruction and got a bird's-eye view. If it wasn't real enough already, coming that close and seeing it made it that much more real. We also went to some of the rescue sites and saw the work that was being done. They were already a couple of levels down and to see all of that debris was just amazing. Seeing it in person made us remember exactly where we were and what we were doing when that happened on September 11.

We were in Milwaukee and I was actually on a fishing boat in Lake Michigan with Bob Uecker, one of the Brewers' announcers. Another boat captain radioed us and told Bob to turn on his radio. When we heard what happened we pretty much forgot about fishing and were glued to the radio. We got a little reception on the TV he had on the boat, and our hearts just sank in disbelief. I began to get a lot of calls on my cell phone from other players, and we were trying to figure out what was going to happen baseball-wise. It became apparent pretty quickly that we were not going to be playing a game that night, and it didn't seem very important. All you could think about was family, and feeling bad for guys like Matt Morris, who has a lot of family in the area. You put yourself in their shoes and it makes a slump or a losing streak not seem so bad.

At ground zero, we saw a lot of memorials and photos of missing people. There were still people searching, hoping they were going to find their loved ones. We realized just how that event had changed the course of everyone's lives forever.

*M. M.*

——— MIKE MATHENY

*W*e finished April only two games under .500, at 12-14, and considering all of the injuries to our pitching staff, I think everyone was pleased. In those 26 games, we used 10 different starting pitchers, including two rookies, Josh Pearce and Travis Smith, and two relievers, Mike Crudale and Mike Timlin.

Part of the reason we were able to get through that stretch was because our pitching coach, Dave Duncan, really works hard to make sure everybody knows we have a plan and what it is. It makes it easier to pitch and catch when you have a clear plan. Today, Smith got his second career start because Garrett Stephenson was hurt. He pitched a week ago, in Montreal, and kept us in the game long enough for us to win it in the 11th inning.

Before that game, and again before today's game, Dunc had a pretty good idea of what his stuff was. We did our scouting and preparation, so we had a pretty good idea of the Florida hitters' weaknesses coming into the game. We had a couple of meetings, and he explained to Travis how he wanted us to pitch their guys. One of the keys is not to make the game plan too confusing or complicated. You have to let the guy know you want him to go with his strengths and just give them a few cues and things to stay away from. You pick out a couple of guys in the lineup who could really hurt you. I think that makes the new pitchers feel a little more comfortable, knowing that they can just come in and pitch their game. They know they should not try to do more than what they are supposed to do, and not try to be a different kind of a pitcher than what they are.

When he joined the club, Travis and I had a chance to sit down and talk. I feel if I can sit down with a guy for 30 minutes I can find out a lot about him. Usually we do it when the team is stretching or during batting practice. Even before I know what the guy's role is going to be, I want to make him tell me how he pitches. I ask him to go through his pitches and tell me the side of the plate he likes to throw to. I want to know what he uses to get right-handers out, what he uses to get ahead, what he likes to do in the middle counts, what he relies on in tough counts, what's his out pitch to a righty or a lefty, what off-speed pitches he goes to in a must-strike situation—everything that could possibly come up during the ballgame.

I make mental notes as we talk. The more information they can give me, the less shaky they will be and the fewer problems we will have in the middle of the game. I always try to end the conversation with them teaching me how they pitch. I feel I'm smart enough that I will catch on before too long. I told Travis and all of the other new guys, "You pitch your game. Don't be afraid to shake me off. Pretty soon we will get together." There are times where every plan is going to change because of the situation. It makes the pitchers more comfortable to know that I've done my work. I've done my scouting and watched film and I tell them I am not going to let them do anything stupid. I tell them, "You can call your game, but in a big situation where something can really hurt us, if there is something that you're trying to do that I don't think is a good idea, I'm going to come out and talk to you about it and tell you why." If they think somebody is back behind the plate working and aware of a situation that could cause them trouble, they have a little extra sense of satisfaction and are a little more comfortable in a tense situation.

Sometimes you can outthink yourself and overanalyze—when less is better than more. Everything clicked today, and Travis did a great job. He shut down the Marlins for six innings, Tino Martinez broke out with two homers, and Travis got his first career win. I hope he had a nice dinner to celebrate, because it was a special day in his life.

*M. M.*

—— MIKE MATHENY

*W*e played an exciting game against the Braves tonight, but it didn't turn out well for us. We lost 2-1 in 11 innings, and all of the fans were second-guessing Tony after we didn't walk Chipper Jones intentionally and he hit a two-run homer off Gene Stechschulte.

It was a tough situation. They had a runner on third with two outs and Chipper coming to bat. Gary Sheffield was on deck. We knew we didn't want to let Chipper beat us, but instead of just walking him, what we wanted to do was pitch him carefully outside the zone and make him be extra aggressive. I've seen it work many times. It's a real pressure point for a pitcher, but it's also a real pressure point for a hitter, especially if it's a guy who feels like he is carrying his team. That definitely fit Chipper in this situation. Sometimes you can use his aggressiveness to get an easy out. We had a meeting on the mound before he came up and decided that was what we were going to try to do, pitch him tough and hope he got a little extra aggressive. We had a clear idea of what we were going to do. We weren't going to give him anything to hit. Gene knew what he wanted to do. He had been our go-to guy in close situations out of the bullpen and had done a great job. The first three pitches were outside and Chipper didn't swing, but the next pitch didn't end up where we wanted it and Chipper swung and hit a home run.

Tony's favorite saying is that we are men, not machines. That was a human mistake. I can take blame for maybe not being as far off the plate as I should have been, but you also have to give credit to a guy for taking a pitch that we didn't think was that bad of a pitch and hitting it out of the ballpark.

When a mistake like that happens the blame usually falls on the manager, but there really should not have been anybody to blame. We had a clear picture of what we were trying to do; we just didn't do it. Second-guessing a decision is the easiest thing to do in baseball. It seems like a lot of the second-guessing in the game comes down to the bullpen, where it usually is obvious if a move doesn't work out.

Handling a bullpen is tough for a manager and a pitching coach because you have so many different personalities to deal with. Some of the guys communicate what their needs are well and some don't, and you are trying to keep everybody at the top of their game. Sometimes you have to read minds. There are guys who will go out there and pitch until their arm falls off and then you've got other guys who will let you know when they come up a little lame. That's an advantage of having a lot of veteran pitchers because they know what makes them go and they know how to communicate with the manager and pitching coach.

Players usually don't talk about whether a move works or doesn't work, because then you get into second-guessing and finger pointing and that can really start breaking apart the chemistry that everyone talks about as being so important on a team. Usually the reflection and conversation afterwards revolve around guys personally feeling what they could have done or should have done. That was what happened tonight. Gene and I talked about it, but what was there really to say? He knew that wasn't where he wanted to make that pitch, and I did too. We've got to be able to make that pitch in that situation, but he doesn't need to hear that. For an intense athlete like Gene, that's not what he wants to hear. I know he is going to be harder on himself than anybody else is going to be.

*JR. JR.*

—— MIKE MATHENY

*D*uring a "normal" season a team might have five or so closed-door meetings. Tony has a pretty good nose for that and he calls most of ours. A couple of days ago, in Chicago, Tino Martinez called one. It was the first time he had spoken up. He just told everybody how we were better than the way we were playing, and I think it picked everybody up.

Another way for a team to get picked up is having the kind of game we had today. The Reds scored six runs in the first inning and we were down 8-0 in the second. It was ugly in a hurry. But what stood out in my mind as I was sitting on the bench was that our base coaches, Jose Oquendo and Dave McKay, kept coming in every inning like we were only down by one run. I don't know if they got together and planned it or were doing it separately. They just both seemed completely confident that we could come back, and we were already down eight runs. Sometimes things like that get overlooked, but I know guys were thriving on it. We weren't giving up, guys were still putting up tough at-bats, and we started to chip away.

J. D. Drew got a two-run single in the fifth as we scored three runs, and we got two more in the sixth to narrow the gap. In the eighth, Placido Polanco drove in two runs and scored the tying run on a hit by Fernando Vina. Everybody in the dugout was going crazy. Then J. D. came up again and hit a two-run homer, and all of a sudden we were ahead 10-8. Izzy came in and got the save. We found out later it was the Cardinals' biggest rally to win a game in 10 years.

I had an opportunity to get interviewed that night, and I said I think a team can ride a comeback like this for weeks. You know you can score runs, and if you are down late in a game, you don't feel like it's insurmountable when you've just come back from 8-0. You get a lot of confidence, because there are a lot of guys who have to do things right to get that to happen. You don't put all of it on one guy's shoulders. You have to collectively get together if you are going to overcome any kind of deficit.

*M. M.*

—— ANDY BENES

*I* have been home for more than a month, and the only time I picked up a baseball was to play catch with my boys in the backyard. I am not actively rehabbing because there really isn't anything I can do.

A few days ago I was on my way to Cape Girardeau to watch my son Drew play in a Little League tournament when I decided to call Walt Jocketty. I was still getting paid and had just gotten a check. I wanted to let him know that if they had any interest in me rehabbing I was willing to do that. They had had so many problems with their starting pitching and had guys like Mike Crudale and Mike Timlin come out of the bullpen to start games. That was not their job. Walt said he needed to talk to Tony and Dave Duncan and find out the situation, and that he would get back to me. I've always had a good relationship with Walt. I have a great deal of respect for what he does.

Today I was pitching underhanded to my son Shane's kindergarten pee-wee team when my cell phone rang. I saw it was someone calling from the stadium, so I said I had to take the call. Another dad jumped in and took over for me.

It was Walt, and he asked me what I was doing. I said I was pitching right now, and he asked, "Great, who are you throwing to?" I said, "My son's T-ball team." And he said, "Are you getting them out?" I told him I was hitting their bats, and I thought that was a good thing.

A really good friend of my wife's had just told her that I was going to pitch again for the Cardinals this year. I thought she was crazy. But Walt said he had talked to Tony and Dunc, and they would like for me to start rehabbing. I had to get back into a throwing program. It doesn't happen over-night. I had been sitting out for a month, so I had lost most of what I had gained in spring training.

Walt told me that as soon as I was ready, I would be going to Memphis, He didn't make any promises. Walt has always been very honest with me, and that is not always the case in baseball. He is a man of his word. He said they wanted me to rehab, get back into shape, and then they would see what happened.

*A. B.*

——— FERNANDO VINA

When you come to the ballpark every day, you never know what to expect. Today I hit a grand slam and drove in five runs as we beat the Pirates 7-3. It was our 12th win in the last 14 games, and being able to contribute in that fashion is a very good feeling.

What you have to keep in perspective, however, is that it feels good and you are happy, but when the game is over, it's over. You just have to store that memory away for later. Because I am not known as a home run hitter, when something like that happens, you enjoy the heck out of it for the day and cherish it, but you can't dwell on it for long, or before you know it you will have played another game and gone 0-4.

(John Heller, AP/Wide World Photos)

Fernando Vina is all intensity as he hammers a two-out grand slam in the second inning to help secure a 7-3 win over the Pirates on May 26.

One of the keys to our club so far has been that different guys keep stepping in and become the star for the day, and today it just happened to be my turn.

*J.V.*

——— JASON ISRINGHAUSEN

*I* have noticed one thing already about our team in the first two months of the season. We have a very good offense, but it seems like we are either hit or miss. We will score 10 runs, or we'll score two. There have not been many games where we score some number in between.

As long as we win, that doesn't bother me at all. Sometimes people try to make a big deal about how often I am pitching. If we win by more than three runs, chances are I won't pitch. As long as we're winning I don't mind if I get 10 saves. What it all depends on is the team's final record. This is a team sport, not an individual sport.

I do like to do my part to contribute to the wins, and this has been a good month. We beat the Astros tonight and I earned my 12th save of the month. Somebody checked and found out it was the most saves I had ever had in a month in my career and tied the major-league record for most saves in May. It also was the most saves in a month by a Cardinal reliever since Lee Smith saved 15 in June of 1993.

I learned a long time ago the number of saves doesn't matter. I have been having some pain in my shoulder and arm, but I know I can pitch through it.

*J. J.*

—— MIKE MATHENY

*A*ll of the talk in baseball is about steroids. Jose Canseco is making a lot of claims about how many people are on steroids, and there was a big story in *Sports Illustrated* that claims Ken Caminiti was using steroids when he won the MVP award a few years ago.

What is discouraging to me is the numbers that are being thrown around without any evidence to back it up. That has scarred all of the players in the game and the game as a whole. It definitely has been a black eye for baseball. There may be guys who are on something, but it's impossible to speculate how many. That's a decision somebody is going to make as an individual, and he isn't going to go around asking guys to

hold the needle for him or inject it for him.
They are not going to talk publicly about it.

What bothers me more than anything
else is to think how it influences kids. You
try to do as much in the community as you
can to be a positive influence for the younger
generation. As professional athletes, we've
been given such a great platform to influence
kids in a positive way. There are so few
people that they will listen to. Because we
wear this jersey for however long we can,
they will listen whether we like it or not. I
know without a doubt that there is a large
number of kids out there who think that
taking steroids is what they need to do to get
to the big leagues, and I am sure that there's
some abuse going on because of what happened. That's a bad thing to think about.

*M. M.*

—— KERRY ROBINSON

*P*inch hitting might be the toughest
thing I've ever done in sports. You go
up there cold, facing bullpen guys most of
the time, and those are guys whose specialty
is getting guys like me out. I always try my
best, but I don't think people realize how
tough it is.

Right now, that's the role I have on this
ball club, to be an extra player and come in
and try to do the best I can when I am called
upon. I thought I had an idea of how I was
going to be used, and I tried to prepare
myself for that, but I got surprised when
Tony [La Russa] didn't always do what I
expected. I have learned to just try to be
ready at all times.

Today I had a break because I got in some at-bats before the game against Rick Ankiel, who is traveling with the ball club as he tries to make his way back to the big leagues. I have been feeling good at the plate, and I think if I had had a chance to play a little more over this two-week stretch I would have been able to post some good results. When I came up to bat in the seventh, I tried to treat it just like another at-bat in the game, and I was lucky enough to hit a home run.

Coming off the bench takes a special kind of mental toughness, and one of the keys to our ball club is that we have been getting good production out of all of the extra guys. We all kind of band together, and about the fifth inning we go to the cage and begin to warm up so that we can be ready whenever we are called upon.

We lost the game, 10-5, stopping a four-game winning streak, but everybody is very positive about the way this season is going.

K.R.

——— MIKE MATHENY

$\mathcal{E}$verybody on the team knew that Jack Buck was in the hospital and was not doing well, which was why I was surprised to see his son Joe in the clubhouse before the game. Joe and I are pretty close, and I had a chance to talk to him. He was very subdued, but he never mentioned anything about his dad. I remember as I saw him that I was thinking that something had probably happened to his dad or else he would still be at the hospital. He was scheduled to broadcast the game that night, but I know they could have had someone fill in for him.

I knew Joe long before I became a Cardinal. My wife Kristin and Joe's wife Ann went to high school together. They came to our

(Tom Gannam, AP/Wide World Photos)

*We were all very sad when Mr. Buck died, but we know he would have been proud of us as we beat the Angels on June 19. Adam Kennedy watches as Placido Polanco rounds the bases after hitting his second home run of the game.*

wedding and we went to theirs. We have spent some time together, so we don't just have a professional relationship, but a personal one as well. He knew the affection I had for his dad and still have.

This turned out to be the night we moved into sole possession of first place in the division. Darryl Kile pitched and we beat the Angels 7-2. It was the first time the Cardinals had ever played the Angels. Joe said later he thought it was really almost a little eerie how his dad had died the night we played the Angels and went into first place, almost like he had been waiting for that to happen.

Moving into first place is always a big thing, but after all we still had more than three months of the season to go, so the team wasn't acting much different than usual after the game. Everybody kind of gets into their own little world thinking about what happened or didn't happen during the game. It wasn't too long before we saw different groups kind of whispering to each other. When you see something like that beginning to stir, you know something is going on, and I think most of us had the assumption that something might have happened with Mr. Buck.

I didn't find out until the next day when Walt Jocketty came up to me that I would be speaking at the memorial service at the ballpark. He said the Buck family had requested that I speak on behalf of the players and the team. I considered it a huge honor, but I wasn't prepared to be asked to do that. I had no idea what I was going to say, but I just relied on my faith to get me through it.

It was amazing to watch the response from the city. I was not surprised. It was interesting to see how many people's lives he had touched and to see the people who came out and spoke up. It was like the whole city shut down for a day. On every radio station people were giving stories about what Mr. Buck had meant to them, about a personal moment they had had with him or how they just knew him via the radio. That one person affected so many people's lives in such a positive way just speaks volumes about the quality of the person that you were talking about.

Everybody on the team was affected by his death, but I think it probably hit Tony harder than most of the players because he and Mr. Buck had really grown close over the past few years. Tony had just lost his own father a few weeks before, and this was an emotional moment for him and all of us.

*M. M.*

JUNE 18, ST. LOUIS

KERRY ROBINSON

*I* know there were probably players on our team who were closer to Jack Buck than I was, but having grown up in St. Louis and having listened to and watched Cardinals baseball all of my life, his death still hit me hard. Pretty much what I know about Cardinals baseball is Jack Buck and Mike Shannon.

He was a wonderful person, and he was always interested in what you had to say. Whenever he was at the ballpark he made it a point to be on the field during batting practice so that he could talk to everybody.

I will never forget the first time I met him and he interviewed me. It was after the 1996 season was over, and I had won the Midwest League batting title playing for the

Cardinals' farm team in Peoria. The Cardinals were still playing, and I came to the game and Jack and Mike had me on the air during the game. It was the highlight of my life, to be interviewed by Jack Buck and Mike Shannon. I couldn't believe I was being interviewed by those guys.

*K. R.*

——— MIKE MATHENY

*A*ny time the Cardinals play the Cubs it is a big deal. It doesn't matter if the two teams are battling for first place, or if one of them is going for the pennant and the other is in last place. Records don't matter, and the fans pack Busch Stadium or Wrigley Field for the games and just have a great time. It is a tremendous atmosphere for baseball.

Today was no exception. It was a sold-out crowd and was going to be Fox's *MLB Game of the Week.*

I first could tell something was wrong when we were doing our stretching before the game. Dave Veres came up to me and said, "Darryl's not here yet." I felt kind of

(James A. Finley, AP/Wide World Photos)

*Our good friend and teammate Darryl Kile pitches against the Angels just days before his death. Darryl died on June 22 in his hotel room in Chicago, and we all miss him very much.*

panicked at that point. There are some guys that if you told me they weren't there for stretching I would have laughed, thinking, "They will be surprised when they wake up and realize it was a day game," but not Darryl Kile. The first thing that came to my mind was that something was wrong. I ran in from the field, which normally I wouldn't do, and ran into the clubhouse and grabbed my cell phone. I called him and left him a message, just telling him I was trying to get ahold of him, that I was worried about him and that I hoped everything was all right. I reminded him about what time we had stretching. I was trying to kind of get him in there quietly and not get him in any trouble.

I was getting ready to leave the club-house and go back out for batting practice when I felt like somebody else needed to

know. I told our trainer, Barry Weinberg, that
Darryl wasn't here and that I was worried. I
asked him to have somebody call his room in
the hotel, and if they couldn't get through, to
get security and go check on him. I found
out later that Dave also had things in motion
with his wife, Robin, and that she was trying
to run things down at the hotel. I don't
know who got there first, but they did get
ahold of security and they went up to check
and found him.

A message had gotten back to Dave from
his wife about some of the comments that
were coming out of the room and she was
pretty worked up. Dave came to me and said,
"Something is going on with Darryl and I
think it's bad. No one's talking. They won't
let us know." Everybody was wandering
around and you could tell there was a lot of

concern. I got the team together and we got down in the middle of the clubhouse. I asked everybody to take a knee because we were going to pray for a minute. I prayed for Darryl and his family for comfort. Then Woody [Williams] prayed and when he finished we all lifted our heads and Tony was standing right there. We were still on our knees and Tony said, "Guys, I just got off the phone with Walt, and they went to Darryl's room and found him dead."

I took off out of the room, went into the trainer's room and tried to find a corner away from everybody else, which in the tiny club-house at Wrigley is hard to do. It was the first cry I've had in a long time. I wasn't paying attention to anybody else, but I imagine that's what everybody did. I've been pretty fortunate in my life that all four of my grandparents are still alive, and this was the first time anybody close to me had passed away. I'm sure I sat there for an hour, going through the whole gamut of emotions. I had a lot of questions like everybody else. All of a sudden I got real tired of being there. I went in the locker room and everybody was still silent. It looked like they were stuck in the same position they had been in for an hour.

I told Tony I just needed to get out of there. He wanted to know where I was going. He had his own issues he was dealing with. A couple of guys told me they had not contacted Darryl's wife Flynn yet, so at that point a few of us starting talking a little more. Obviously, the game was canceled. We all got on the bus as quick as we could and went back to the hotel. Fortunately my wife and a lot of the other wives were there. We walked down to Lakeshore Drive and sat on the beach.

We all got together again later at the hotel, and it was good. We had the employee assistance people come in and Walt Enoch and Rick Horton from Baseball Chapel were there. Most of all it was a time for us to talk. Tony opened up the floor, Dave Duncan followed and then other guys talked. It went on for a while. They told us later that night we were going to have a service the next morning. We talked about whether to play the next night. Tony left the decision up to us. Nobody had had much experience with a situation like that. It seemed like the right thing to do, to go ahead and play.

That night everybody went their separate ways. I checked out of the hotel; I didn't really want to stay there. I got a room at the hotel across the street.

I never really saw Darryl's death as a test of my faith. I saw it as a difficult circumstance in life, and something I had not had to face up to that point. I believe that God is in control, and that things all happen for a purpose. It was an extremely difficult day.

M. M.

MIKE MATHENY

*W*hen the team was talking at the hotel last night, I didn't say much when the vote came on whether to play the game tonight or not. My heart and my mind really weren't there. I debated over what to do. For the first time ever in my career I went in and asked not to play.

Tony said he was going to talk to me first before he made out the lineup because he knew the relationship Darryl and I had. It was Darryl's day to pitch, and Darryl had always told me, "If you're not catching, I'm not pitching." I told Tony the same thing. "Out of respect for Darryl, I feel since he's not pitching, I'm not catching." It was my hope that he could respect that, and, of

(Stephen Carrera, AP/Wide World Photos)

We cancelled the game against the Cubs on Saturday when we found out about Darryl, but we played on Sunday because that is what we thought he would have wanted. Before the game, we all observed a moment of silence for Darryl. Our hearts and minds were not in the game and we lost to the Cubs.

course, he did. It was a tough day. I admire the guys for going out and playing. I hope they don't feel I copped out on them. I'm sure they were wondering if playing was the right thing to do because none of their minds were in it either.

The Cubs won 8-3. All we wanted to do was get on the plane and get out of there and go home.

We have an off day tomorrow, but then we have to play again. There are positives and negatives in that the game goes on. The off day will help, but we won't really have a chance to stop and reflect until the All-Star break, when we can get away and go fly-fishing for trout or something. Darryl was definitely on my list of all-time great team-mates, and I know that was true for almost everybody in our ball club.

*M. M.*

———— MIKE MATHENY

We had a memorial service for Darryl at the ballpark today. It gave us a chance to put a little closure to it. It was gratifying to see how many players and personnel came in from other teams, because it just showed you all of the lives Darryl had touched. We got to spend time with Flynn and the kids.

The baseball world was definitely impacted by Darryl's death. We all realized how fragile life is, and a lot of us realized we're not invincible. Athletes sometimes think we are above a lot of things because we are treated so well. Darryl's death was so sudden, with no warning, and it made people all over the world stop and look at what's important, and where you should invest your time. A lot of guys went home and spent a lot of quality time with their family.

After the service, I think for the first time, a lot of the guys felt it was time to go on with the game. Woody talked during the service and he was pitching. Both of us were extremely fired up for the game. He pitched a gem. I wanted to do something special. The same thing happened after Mr. Buck's ceremony, too. I wanted to shine that day and ended up having a pretty good game. For the first time since April I drove in two runs in a game and had three hits. Woody pitched great and we beat Milwaukee 5-2.

Kannon, Darryl's little boy, threw out the first pitch and got to hang around with us during the game. Matt [Morris] and Jason [Isringhausen] had him doing all kinds of things. Nobody could look at him without smiling, but your heart was breaking at the same time.

Nobody knows what the long-term effect of losing Darryl will be on the team. People are already starting to give us excuses if we lose. We aren't going to be looking for excuses. When it's time to play, we will play, and do everything we can to win. We're also human, and off the field we will deal with the things we have to deal with. When we come out to play nobody will be focused on anything negative. It's one of the things I already have been amazed about with this team. Guys could respond in a number of different ways, but I expect us to have a very positive attitude. It didn't give us an extra spark or motivation. It's just going to be a matter of guys going out and doing what we know how to do best—play baseball.

*JT. JT.*

—— MATT MORRIS

*I*t's always an honor to make the All-Star team, but this year there was just no way I felt like playing.

I was just worn out. I wanted a break like the rest of the guys. Even if I had been 100 percent physically, I don't think I would have been there mentally. We were all so close to Darryl, and his death affected all of us so much. One of the things that happened to me is that I lost about 20 pounds from where I was in spring training. I was down to about 200 pounds, which I've pitched at before, but that's really light for me. With everything that had been going on, I just overlooked eating. I never felt hungry, my stomach was in knots, and I had other things on my mind. I just felt weak.

Being physically worn down with a lot of little aches and pains made it an easier decision not to pitch. I just didn't think trying to throw those extra pitches and then go back and try to help the team win was a good idea. We had reached the All-Star break in first place, with a two-game lead, but we all knew we had a long second half of the season to play.

My fiancee, Heather, is from Wisconsin, and my parents came out so we had a chance to be together for a couple of days and get away from the hotel scene. That was a nice break.

Even though I wasn't going to be pitching in the game, I still wanted to attend the game and be introduced with the rest of the players. Heather and I talked about doing something to honor Darryl, but I wasn't sure what to do. I thought about wearing his jersey, number 57, instead of 35. I wanted to honor him, but I didn't want to draw too much attention to it again, either. I decided a couple of days beforehand to write his initials DK on one palm and his number 57 on the other in ink, so when I was introduced I held up my palms for the national television audience. I had to be careful not to mark myself up too early, however, because everybody was going around shaking hands and I didn't want to mark up any jerseys.

I knew then that every time I went out on the mound to pitch, DK would always be with me. We called him the curveball master. I went to school with him, so to speak. He was always teaching. We would throw the ball every day, loosening up in the outfield before games, and flip curveballs at each other. He was always watching me and telling me what I was doing wrong or praising me for the ones I did right. One of the best pieces of advice I ever got was from him, and it was about how to make my curveball look. He was talking about not just how to throw it, but how the hitters saw it coming out of my hand. That kind of got me over the edge about how to use my curveball. He taught me to throw it low enough to make it look like a fastball. That's what a hitter is always geared for, and from that point on, my curve was always breaking down. It really helped make me a better pitcher.

As I looked back on the first half of the season, there were some games that I "easily" could have won, or at least had a chance to win because our offense scored a bunch of runs and put me ahead, but I didn't do my job. Games where I make physical mistakes are one thing, but I really question myself after games where I feel I let down mentally, and that happened a lot during the middle of the season.

*M. M.*

—— MIKE MATHENY

*C*huck Finley is going to make his Busch Stadium debut tonight, and I hope he is as excited about it as we are to have him on the team. Our GM, Walt Jocketty, acquired him in a trade from Cleveland, and I think he will be a major help to our pitching staff. He made his first start for us last weekend in Pittsburgh and showed he has got a lot left.

It's fun to see the energy that comes from making a move like that. Believe me, the players notice when the front office is willing to make a move to help give us a chance to win. Watching the teams maneuvering, especially when the trade deadline is approaching, is like watching a chess game, seeing which teams make the first moves and what other teams do to counter them.

It gets the fans excited, too, because they can see that the front office is serious about us making a run for it. I've been on the other end of it, too. One year in Milwaukee we were coming up on the deadline and thought we had a legitimate chance of making a run for the pennant. We were looking at what we could do, and what other teams were doing, and we did absolutely nothing.

There is a lot of talk going around that we might make a deal for Scott Rolen from the Phillies, which has everybody pretty excited. You can thrive off the energy a new guy like Finley or Rolen can bring to a team.

It's really fun to watch the new guys come in and see their reaction to playing as a Cardinal at Busch Stadium. You can see it in their face and eyes. Tonight we had the largest crowd of the year, more than 48,000 against the Cubs. Finley pitched and we won 8-4. When you have the excitement that we have in our stands, it really does extend to the players. It doesn't happen anywhere like it does at Busch.

*JT. JT.*

—— FERNANDO VINA

*O*ne of the keys to being a good club is
trying to make the season as smooth as
possible. You know there are going to be
highs and lows, and if you can try not to get
too excited about the highs and too depressed
about the lows, you remember that over 162
games things usually even out.

Tonight was one of the highs, and it
was really hard not to get too excited. We
were playing the Cubs on *Sunday Night
Baseball* on ESPN, and we came back from a
6-0 deficit to win the game 10-9 on Edgar
Renteria's three-run walk-off homer in the
bottom of the ninth. It seemed everybody on
our team made a contribution to the win, but
Edgar was the star, and I was happy for him.

Edgar and I have been teammates for the past three years, and we have developed a very good relationship. He is a great guy and a special person. We were able to mesh well from the beginning, which is important for a shortstop and a second baseman. He is a big-hearted guy, and we have the same type of characteristics. I think we are both very serious about the game, and we work hard to be the best players we can be. We live in the same complex, so we often eat lunch together and go out of our way to help each other out. We both realize defense is just as important as offense, and it is something we take a lot of pride in. It sometimes gets overlooked, but we certainly notice when the other guy makes a great defensive play.

Tonight he was the hero on offense and everybody noticed, and I was proud of him. It was a big win for our club.

*J.V.*

───── ANDY BENES

*W*hen I decided to come back, I really knew that my attitude was totally going to affect how things went. If my attitude was good I knew things were going to be OK. If it was bad I knew I would be wasting my time. I decided that when I went to Memphis, I wasn't just going to go in and do my work and leave and come back four days later. I was going to go there, be on the team, be a good teammate and be a part of what was going on. I was excited to be there.

I had about 10 days left in my rehab and the All-Star break was coming up, and it looked like I was only going to get one more start. We worked it out so that I could pitch in Potomac, then I would get my last start in

*90*

Memphis before my rehab was over. I was going there when the Cardinals called and said they wanted me to join them in San Diego for the start of the second half.

I was excited for the opportunity. I knew I had a good attitude going, and I was going about my job the right way. I started a game at Los Angeles, pitched in relief in Pittsburgh and started at San Francisco, but I had not gotten a win. Against the Giants I had two outs in the fifth, we were leading 2-0, and then somebody made an error and Tony took me out of the game. I knew then I was going to have to earn Tony's confidence and respect back because of the way I had pitched the last year and a half. I told myself that it was not personal.

I just looked at it like it was a game-to-game situation. I kind of viewed my role as filling in for DK for the rest of the season, and I wanted to do the best I could do.

We had made a trade for Chuck
Finley, and I watched the way he pitched. He
had a great split-finger fastball, and I started
talking with him about it. He showed me
how he held it, and we played catch in the
outfield. He told me he thought it could be a
good pitch for me. When I was throwing in
the bullpen I told Dunc about it, because I
felt I needed something else. Going into
tonight's game at Florida, that's all I had
thrown it, but I decided to use it if the situation called for it in the game.

I wasn't going to hold anything back. I
used it to get some really big outs. I pitched
six and one-third innings and retired 10 of
the last 11 batters I faced. I won my first
game in nearly a year. I told the press after
the game that there were times I didn't know
if I would make it back, but that my attitude
was good and that I really looked at each

game as an opportunity and that was all I could ask for. That was exactly how I felt.

I felt good about the way I was pitch-ing and thought the split-finger could be a good pitch for me. It was a pitch I could throw for strikes, and it could do for me what my change-up had done in the past. And it was all because a teammate had taken the time to help me with it.

We were in first place, leading our division by five games. It was exciting, and it was fun to feel like I was part of it.

*A. B.*

―――― MIKE MATHENY

We lost our seventh game in a row tonight, falling to Montreal. All of a sudden we have stopped hitting. Our lead is down to one game, but I don't think anybody is panicking. We have a good club, and even the best clubs go through streaks like this. The better the team is, the shorter the streak.

We have good leadership on this team, and we will come out of this slump. We have a bunch of guys who have been close before, and we know we are going to be close again. Getting close makes a team hungry to win. It's fun playing on a team where a bunch of the guys are used to winning. My locker is next to Tino Martinez, and we talk all the time. I've been picking his brain all year because he just has so much experience.

We know we will be close this year, and we just want to have the opportunity to finish it off. You don't see as much selfishness on a team like that. We know we will have a chance to achieve our goal, and that is to win it all.

*M. M.*

(Gene J. Puskar, AP/Wide World Photos)

Three of our biggest sluggers, J.D. Drew (left), Albert Pujols (center) and Jim Edmonds celebrate after scoring on a ninth-inning double by Tino Martinez. We scored six runs in the ninth to beat the Pirates 11-5 on August 15.

AUGUST 20, ST. LOUIS

—— MIKE MATHENY

*M*y shoulder hasn't felt right most of the season. It never has struck me as a big deal or something I couldn't play with, because it would be abnormal if something wasn't hurting by this point in the season. Guys, especially catchers, play with shoulder pain almost all of the time from the constant foul balls, et cetera. I don't think it has affected my hitting or my throwing, but there are some days it feels better than others. I have tried to maintain my program of lifting weights throughout the season, not to get stronger but so that I can maintain where I want to be, but I finally went in and told our strength and conditioning coach that I wasn't going to be able to lift anymore.

My shoulder has been bothering me while I've been lifting, and I think we are far enough along in the season that I can ride out the rest of the season without lifting. It was his responsibility to tell the trainers, and they kind of panicked when they heard my shoulder was hurt. There wasn't anything specific to tell them, and I am glad they respected the fact that I told them I would get with them and see what we could find out at the end of the year.

If the pain had been so bad that I thought it was affecting my performance and the performance of the team it would have been different. Most of the throws a catcher makes during a game, however, are really just lobs back to the pitcher. I could feel the pain more when I was playing catch, but I also thought I was strengthening my arm. Every season it seems you go through a couple of stretches where your mechanics are off, but in the games when I needed to make a hard throw and let it go, the ball was already gone before I would feel any pain. There usually are only about 10 times a night you really have to let it go.

I take a lot of pride in my defense and throwing. In 2000, getting a chance to play and being able to throw out some guys trying to steal turned the tide in some games.

That helped me get some respect among the pitching staff. We were able to get them an easy out, and once you get a sense of that and realize the confidence that they put in you, that's something you want to keep going.

*M. M.*

(Tom Gannam, AP/Wide World Photos)

*Edgar Renteria (center) and Albert Pujols
(left) celebrate with Vina after his double
sealed the win over the Pirates on August 22.*

## AUGUST 22, ST. LOUIS

———— FERNANDO VINA

$\mathcal{I}$t has been amazing to me how well we have continued to play despite everything we have gone through this season. Tonight was another example. We were losing to Pittsburgh 4-2 going into the ninth inning, but Tino Martinez led off with a double and scored on a single by Edgar Renteria. Miguel Cairo came up with a pinch-hit single, and I followed that with a double that drove in both runs and we won the game 5-4.

What happened to this club was something that I wouldn't want to wish on anybody. I didn't really know how to play through it. My perspective and my responsibility toward the game were kind of lost. It was my job, but we just kind of lost every-thing outside of the people we love. My motivation and my fire to play the game is so important to me, and I had to dig deep to find it. You realize there are so many other things that are more important.

In the days and weeks after Darryl died, our minds weren't on playing the game. I wasn't focused the way I am supposed to be when I am playing. As time went on we were able to talk as a team and we knew what Darryl would want us to do. He would want us to win. That helped us put the games in perspective, and we had an attitude of "let's go out and play hard and do what we need to do." That's the approach we took tonight, when it would have been easy to go out 1-2-3 in the ninth and have the game be over. We didn't do that, and that is why I am so proud of this team and my teammates.

You can never get away from what happened and you always wonder why. There are so many questions unanswered from God up above. I always tell myself that everything happens for a reason and that Darryl is in a better place. God just wanted him with Him then, and we have to accept that and go on.

*F.V.*

—— MATT MORRIS

*W*e played the Phillies tonight, and I hung a curveball that Mike Lieberthal hit into the seats to tie the game. That wasn't the worst thing that happened.

In my next at-bat after his homer, I hit a routine ground ball. I was stubborn and ran as hard as I could to try to beat it out, even though I had no chance. I ended up re-aggravating a hamstring injury and am going to go on the disabled list tomorrow.

I hurt it last week, in Philadelphia, when I pitched on a really hot day. The Phillies were honoring Harry Kalas, their longtime announcer, and it was a sellout crowd. I was dehydrated because of the heat, and I twinged my hamstring running to first.

I knew as soon as it happened tonight that I was going to be out awhile. I didn't want to miss time, I don't think any player or pitcher does, but injuries are part of the game.

At the beginning of the season, DK, Woody [Williams] and I kind of made up a contest of challenging ourselves on who was going to lead the staff in strikeouts, ERA and things like that. I think most pitching staffs do it. We come up with some kind of pot that one guy will win at the end of the year. What I really cared most about at that point in the year, however, was trying to pitch well for myself and really finish strong.

I was kind of ashamed of the way I had pitched in the middle of the season, when everything kind of got away from me a little bit. It's hard not being able to do the one thing you can almost always do, or at least compete well, and that's what happened to me. As I mentioned earlier, losing games because I don't physically execute is one thing, but to let myself down mentally really wears on me.

The only good thing somebody said to me was that maybe this time off would make me a little more rested for the playoffs. I hope that's the case. We can't really be thinking about the playoffs yet, with more than a month to play in the regular season, but we are in first with a four-game lead. We've just got to keep it going.

*M. M.*

08
27

—————— KERRY ROBINSON

*W*e acquired Jeff Fassero from Chicago a couple of days ago to help strengthen our bullpen, and I thought it was a good move. I didn't think about it at the time, but when he joined the team in Cincinnati, I found out we both wore uniform number 13.

One of our assistant equipment guys, Rip Rowan, came up to me and said that Jeff wanted to know if I would switch numbers with him. It never really was a big deal for me. I wasn't all that fond of 13. When I had signed back with the Cardinals as a minor-league free agent a couple of years ago, I asked if I could have any number that was under 50. Thirteen was the only one that was available, so I said I would take it. I went to spring training and made the club, so I kept the number.

My favorite number is 15, but Jim Edmonds has that number so I know I'm not getting it. As long as I was changing, I thought I might try a single number and o was the only one available. I got permission to wear it. It's not really a big deal. I find I do watch and root for a couple of guys playing college basketball who also wear o. I'm happy with it.

*K.R.*

(David Kohl, AP/Wide World Photos)

*Pinch hitting may be the toughest job Kerry Robinson ever had to do, but he is great at it. This three-run double against the Reds on August 28 helped us win 9-2.*

—— MIKE MATHENY

*T*he plane ride from Cincinnati to Chicago last night was strange. Today is the day the players' association has set as the strike deadline if we do not have a new agreement with the owners. Our game would be the first one affected, and I think everybody spent the night wondering if we had played our final game of the season and if all of the work we have put in to this point would be lost.

We were pretty much consumed by the strike talk, especially those of us who had kept on top of the issues and on top of the whole process and where the whole thing was going. We knew that whatever happened was going to directly influence our immediate future. We didn't know if we were going to be heading home or how long we were going to be there. We didn't know what a strike would mean to our long-term future or for the good of the game.

Going back to Chicago had everybody pretty tense anyway. It was the first time we had been back there since Darryl's death, and luckily our traveling secretary, C. J. Cherre, had arranged for us to stay at a different hotel. That at least made it kind of a different setting, and we at least had a lot of distraction because of all the strike talk.

It came right down to the wire. We were at the hotel having conference calls and waiting to see what would happen. We weren't going to get on the bus to go to Wrigley until we knew what had happened at the talks in New York. We were just hoping the negotiations would continue and that it wouldn't get to the point where one side would push the other side away. Having been through the strike in 1994, when I didn't really understand the issues that well, I was trying to explain everything to the younger players. That's a time when a team grows closer.

When we got the good news that there would not be a strike, we jumped on the bus. Once we got to the stadium, we knew it was going to be odd to be back there—and it was. It was something we knew we were going to have to face sooner or later. Every-where we went people brought it up; it was like we never had a chance to get away from it.

Especially today, everybody in the media wanted to talk about Darryl and what it was like being back at Wrigley for the first time. It was frustrating. It almost made me start seeing the media in a different light. There wasn't as much of a personal concern involved as there was a feeling that they needed to get the story at all costs. There was no concern for the people who were so closely involved, and that bothered me.

It was very personal to me because Darryl was such a close friend. I didn't feel like I owed anything to the media, and I think most guys felt the same way.

We had a good day on the field. Albert Pujols hit a three-run homer in the first and we won 6-3.

*M. M.*

AUGUST 30, CHICAGO

—— KERRY ROBINSON

All of the players were worried about whether we were going to go on strike or not. It was a scary time for a player of my caliber because if we go on strike for maybe a year, there's nothing to say I'm going to have a job when we come back. It was frustrating from that standpoint, but I was willing to stick with the union as far as it was going to go. Luckily we got the word that the two sides had reached a deal and there would be no strike.

About the only thing that took my mind off thinking about the strike was that we had our fantasy football draft last night. That broke some of the tension. I think I have a good fantasy team, but we will have to see how the season goes.

*K. R.*

# SEPTEMBER 13, HOUSTON

#### JASON ISRINGHAUSEN

*A*t the beginning of the year I always set my sights on 30 saves. That's a good round number to shoot for, and if I can get to that total and keep my blown saves to a minimum (less than five or so), I'm pretty happy with that. I got my 30th save tonight as we beat Houston 3-2 in 10 innings.

I know I could have had more saves. My arm has been in need of repair for about half of the season, and I spent a short time on the disabled list. I am going to have to have surgery when the year is over. I could probably have had four or five more saves throughout the second half if I had been available, but we have a big enough lead in the division that they want to rest me so I can be available every day during the play-offs.

*116*

There are maybe 10 guys in the majors who will finish the year with more saves than me, but a lot of them will be sitting at home watching us when the playoffs begin. That's why the total number of saves doesn't really mean much.

The one game this season that still haunts me was May 30 against the Reds, when I gave up five runs without getting an out. That only happened one time, but if I could have gone through the year without it happening even once, my ERA would be a few points lower and it would have been a better year. Those are the things I think about when I look back on the year. Those are the things that stick in your mind that you know you can improve on. Games that go right seem to disappear really quickly, but the ones that go bad are the ones that stick in your mind for a while.

We know the games that really count are the playoffs, and we're starting to gear up because we can sense it coming. It's what we play for all season, and this team is going to be ready for the challenge.

*J. J.*

MIKE MATHENY

*W*e clinched the division tonight with a win over the Astros. I've been fortunate in that this is the third time I've been able to celebrate, but I've got to admit this was different. You begin the year with the goal of getting to September with something to play for, and we've done that. When you can get into October then you can take your chances.

One of the things that I think was different was that a lot of the guys in the room had also been in this position before and we realized there was still a long way to go. All of the guys who had been through this knew there were a lot of things we still had to do before we could really celebrate.

Still, we had a reason to be happy. There are so many guys who play their entire careers and never have the opportunity to play in the playoffs.

It was yet another moment in the season when we also looked back on everything we had been through as a team. It was definitely a time of reflection and thinking about those who weren't there with us: Darryl, Mr. Buck, Tony's dad and others. Me and the guys had a lot on our minds, and we knew our work for the year was not over.

*M. M.*

—— ANDY BENES

*I* had been pitching really well since coming back into the rotation in July. Since winning in Florida on July 30, I had made 10 starts and only once had I allowed three runs in a game. I was 4-1 in those games, but more importantly, the team was 7-3 in those 10 games.

We had already clinched the division, but were battling the Diamondbacks for home field advantage in the first round of the playoffs. Tony told me that if the game meant something, meaning we still had a possibility to get the home field advantage, that I would start on the final game of the season against Milwaukee. If it didn't mean anything, I wasn't going to pitch.

That really left me with a strange feeling, because I really wanted to pitch. I knew it was going to be my final game in the regular season. I had my mind made up that I was going to retire.

I had pitched against Arizona a few days earlier and had shut them out for seven innings, but we hadn't scored either. I also had 1,998 strikeouts for my career, and for whatever reason I couldn't get those last two strikeouts against Arizona that I needed to get to 2,000. Selfishly, I really wanted to get those two strikeouts.

It turned out the game did mean something, so I started. I struck out the first batter of the game, my 1,999th strikeout. I was having back spasms, and it turned out that I only pitched five innings, and the last batter I faced, Ryan Christenson, became my 2,000th strikeout victim.

I came up to bat in the bottom of the inning, and they flashed it on the scoreboard that I had just struck out the 2,000th batter of my career. I just really thought it was a blessing from the Lord that that was the last pitch I threw in my career in the regular season. It was really special the way it happened.

The crowd gave me a standing ovation, and it was very emotional for me. The fans had been so supportive of me, even when I was going through the tough times. It just turned out that one of the most special things that happened to me in any part of my career turned out to be the last thing that happened to me. I will always remember that.

I didn't know what would happen in the playoffs, because I didn't know if Woody [Williams] was going to be healthy enough to pitch or not. I thought it might have been my last game, but I was hoping I would get another chance.

We won the game, but it turned out Arizona won too, so we had to get on the plane and fly to Phoenix to open the first round. We all were confident that it didn't matter where we played or who we played; we all thought we were going to win.

*A. B.*

## OCTOBER 1, PHOENIX

—— MATT MORRIS

 henever I am going to start the game I always take the bus from the hotel to the ballpark. It is probably the latest we're allowed to get there. I try to waste the day and not get to the park early, so that I won't sit around and think too much.

I was leaving for the ballpark and came down to the hotel lobby and saw Flynn Kile. I wasn't sure she was going to be there, but I thought she might show up. She lives in San Diego, and that's a real short plane trip to Phoenix. I think it was kind of meant to be for me to see her at the hotel instead of noticing her later in the crowd, or finding out afterwards that she was there. It was just really cool.

It was nice knowing that she was there, sitting with the rest of the wives, just like old times. I know everybody was thrilled to see her.

I didn't pitch as well as I did last year in the playoffs in Phoenix, but we were able to get to Randy Johnson and score some runs. I knew if were able to get to him we were going to win. The offense won the game for us, and that was fine with me.

*M. M.*

(James A. Finley. AP/Wide World Photos)

*When Chuck Finley joined the team, he brought a lot of power, consistency and experience to our pitching staff and helped fill the void left by Darryl's death.*

—— FERNANDO VINA

*I* get so excited for playoff-atmosphere
games. It is amazing what they do to
you and how they affect you. The pressure is
incredible, but that's the way I like it. I can't
imagine playing a meaningless game with no
emotion. That's just not my style of baseball.

I knew exactly what I wanted to do to
get our series against the Diamondbacks off
to a good start. My job is to help the team
win, and the way I can do that is by getting
on base and being a pest to the other team,
giving our guys in the middle of the lineup a
chance to drive me in. That's what I did
tonight, and when it works out the way you
want, it's very rewarding.

We knew going into this series that we had a tough challenge, simply because we have to face two of the best pitchers in the game, Randy Johnson and Curt Schilling, back to back. We had to do it last year too, so we know what we are up against. I wanted to get it started right from the beginning.

I got three hits and we bombed Johnson 12-2. Jim Edmonds and Scott Rolen both hit two-run homers. Everybody was excited, but we know it was only one win and we have two more to go. The bottom line is if you're going to achieve something, you've got to see it first, and we knew exactly what we wanted to do in this series.

I could see it before we started that we were all focused on what we needed to do to win. All the pieces were there, and we thought they were all coming together at just the right time. Sometimes you can put too much pressure on yourself and you end up going backwards instead of forward, but we were aware of that because of our experience the last couple of years and I think we were prepared for it.

With everything we have going for us, we believe good things are going to happen.

*F.V.*

―――― MIGUEL CAIRO

Sitting on the bench, you always have to be ready. Usually Tony is going to call on me to pinch hit, but today I came into the game because of an injury to Scott Rolen.

The good thing about being here is that Tony uses all of his players and keeps everyone fresh. The regulars get a day off to rest and we [all of the bench players] get enough chances to play that we are ready.

Nobody wanted to see Scott get hurt. He was fielding a ground ball when one of the Arizona runners collided with him. Scott hurt his shoulder, and right now no one knows how long he is going to be out. We just have to fill in for him like we have done for the other guys all year.

I try to be the best at my job, and I work hard at it. Today I got lucky. My single in the ninth inning drove in Edgar Renteria and we won 2-1, taking a 2-0 lead in the best-of-five series.

I always get ready to pinch hit. I was looking for a fastball to hit hard somewhere. I got a fastball right in the middle. I tried to hit it through the middle. I got lucky. When you're pinch hitting, you're just going to see one good fastball or one strike. Sometimes you're going to miss it. Sometimes you're going to hit it.

Today I got it. And I was glad I hit it where there was no one. Today was a beautiful day for me, and the team too.

I am just blessed right now. I'm in the best organization in baseball. Since I've been here, they've been so good to me. They've been treating me so well. Everybody on this team has been making contributions all year. It's exciting to beat Schilling and Johnson and win two games here, and now we're going home.

*M. C.*

——— MIKE MATHENY

It was a great feeling to get on the plane and fly back from Arizona knowing we were ahead two games to none in the series. It was set up nice where we could clinch at home and not have to worry about Curt Schilling and Randy Johnson again. We didn't have a master plan, but I think all of us knew that having to face those two guys again would not be good. Beating them once was hard enough; having to do it twice would be a much tougher task. We knew that this was the night we had to do it.

We fell behind 2-0, but everyone was still confident. Andy [Benes] was pitching, and he had done such a great job for us the second half of the season that we knew he was going to keep us in the ballgame. We were tied, but then in the fourth I got a single after Miguel Cairo was hit by a pitch. Andy laid down a perfect squeeze bunt, Fernando [Vina] followed with a hit and I scored. We were up 4-2, added a couple of more runs and won 6-3. Cairo came through filling in for Scott [Rolen] and did a great job the entire series. That was what happened all year, guys taking advantage of opportunities when they had the chance.

It was nice to beat Arizona, since they were the team that had knocked us out last year. I don't think it could have been any sweeter, no matter who we were playing. We had our goals set. Everybody on the team might give you a different perspective, but I think getting into the NL Championship Series was very satisfying. There was a good focus in the clubhouse that there were still a couple of more things we needed to do. Our season still seemed incomplete. I was glad to see that the guys weren't content yet, because we were still playing.

*J̃l. J̃l.*

(James A. Finley, AP/Wide World Photos)

*We all go crazy on the field in St. Louis after we swept the defending world champion Arizona Diamondbacks in the National League Division Series on October 5.*

—— MIKE MATHENY

Sweeping Arizona gave us a chance to rest for a few days before we began the series against the Giants. I was one of the guys who needed to let their body heal, but when the series started, we were ready to play again.

It didn't take long for the tone of the series to be set. Matt [Morris] was a little too strong and the Giants roughed him up a little. Kenny Lofton hit a home run in the third, and by the time he came up again in the fifth inning, the Giants were ahead 7-1. Mike Crudale had just come in to relieve Matt.

On the first pitch, Lofton reacted like we were trying to hit him in the head. He started to make a move toward the mound, and whenever that happens I'm going to step in. I don't know if he was going to charge, but I tried to get in a position where I could stop him if he did. He started yelling at me, thinking I had called the pitch. That was what I was trying to do. I wanted his attention on me instead of on the pitcher. I did my job.

It wasn't a beanball. It missed him by a foot and a half. It was inside, but we pitch inside a lot. People in the stands and watching on television could tell I was yelling back at him, but honestly I don't remember what I said. He was saying a lot of things. A long time ago when I learned the basics of catching, I was taught that nobody gets to your pitcher. That's all I was trying to do.

The Giants ended up winning 9-6, and I know Matt really felt he let the team down. Normally six runs should be more than enough to win with him pitching, but it didn't happen tonight. That's the way the game goes. He is such an intense player, and you never, ever want to try to take that away from him. What happens sometimes is when he tries to throw even harder, his ball doesn't move as much. That was what happened tonight. He wanted to pitch so well and his arm felt so good that he threw harder, and the ball flattened out and stayed up in the zone. It's hard to realize in a situation like tonight that you don't have to do that. He has a phenomenal arm and such great stuff that he doesn't have to reach back for something extra. He's had so many big games where he could not have thrown any better, and tonight just didn't happen to go his way.

We're down by one game, but our confidence is as strong as ever.

*π. π.*

—— MATT MORRIS

*B*ecause we swept Arizona, I went eight days between starts before open-ing the League Championship Series against the Giants. I've always been a guy who thrives on adrenaline, and sometimes I've had a problem with being too ready for a game. That's been a problem my whole career. In the situations where everything is bigger and more meaningful, I tend to let that get into my system a little bit.

That's what happened tonight. I let it get away from me. DK always said that it was good to have adrenaline, but you have to know when to use it. Usually my ball is up in the strike zone no matter how hard I throw, but I get hurt when I overthrow. No matter how hard I throw it, guys are going to hit it or I am going to walk them. Location was a big problem.

Nobody has to tell me the first game of any playoff series is a pivotal game. You always want to get that first win under your belt, especially when you are playing at home, so that you are not playing catch-up. We had the chance to do that tonight, but it didn't happen. We scored enough runs to win, so it wasn't even like I had to pitch a shutout for us to win. If I had contained them even a little bit we could have won, and I think we would have easily been on track to win the series.

*M. M.*

OCTOBER 10, ST. LOUIS

───── MIKE MATHENY

*T*onight was just a case of us running into a tremendous pitching performance. Jason Schmidt is a quality pitcher, and he gave us more than we could handle. It was a shame we were not able to get any offense going against him, because Woody [Williams] came out there for us and also turned in a terrific game.

Woody had not pitched in 20 days, and the training staff did a great job just to get him out there. He was still hurting, but he knew we needed him to take the ball. That's the kind of competitor he is. He only gave up three runs in six innings and definitely gave us a chance to win the game, but we couldn't come through.

(Al Behrman, AP/Wide World Photos)

*Tony La Russa and our pitching coach Dave Duncan are already strategizing for Game 2 against the Giants as our hopes for winning Game 1 fade.*

The key guy for the Giants, other than Schmidt, was Rich Aurilia, who hit two home runs. He wasn't the guy we thought was going to beat us.

When you talk about a game plan against the Giants, there is no big secret. You don't want to let Barry Bonds beat you. You have that kind of player on almost every team, and you know going in that when you get in a tough situation with him at the plate you are going to pitch him tough. Whatever you do, don't give in to him. He has earned that respect because he has beaten everybody in clutch situations. When you pick out a guy like that, one thing you know is you also can't give in to the guy hitting behind him, in this case Benito Santiago. You know that if you pitch around Barry you are going to be giving Benito a chance to beat you.

We didn't take Santiago lightly by any means, but you've got to look at what Barry has done in the past. You play the numbers and you play the percentages. You do what you think gives your team the best chance of winning. If you challenge Barry Bonds, the odds are you are going to lose. We challenged him when we could, and tonight he went zero for three with a walk. But in a situation where the game is on the line and he can change the tone of the entire game or even the series, why would you let him do that? Santiago didn't hurt us either, as he went zero for four. But as we saw tonight, you can't take anybody who is a major-league hitter lightly.

The next three games are in San Francisco, and the simple math says we have to
win two of the three to bring the series back
to St. Louis. That's what we are going out
there to do.

*M. M.*

——— MIKE MATHENY

*W*e had a great surprise waiting for us when we arrived. Our buddy Kannon Kile was here. All of the guys are so fond of him. He was around all the time with Darryl, and I think having him come to the game was more of a thrill for us than it was for him. Looking back on it later, I think it will mean more to him than it did today. He was introduced to the crowd, and the Giants' fans gave him a great ovation. That was a real class act on their part. They treated him so well, and it was a special thing to see. He was so excited and into the game.

Kannon got to see a good game. We started out playing awful; it was just a comedy of errors and I didn't know what was

going on. It was amazing that Chuck [Finley]
kept his composure and kept making his
pitches. I was just glad we had a veteran
pitcher on the mound, or things could really
have started falling apart. He was at least
showing that he had confidence in his defense, and we were finally able to get over
our fielding troubles and start making some
plays.

For the first time in the series we were
able to put some hits together. We hit three
solo homers and won the game 6-4, surviving
a three-run homer by Barry Bonds, to cut the
Giants' lead in the series to two games to
one.

I was fortunate to have hit one of the
homers, along with Eli Marrero and Jim
Edmonds. Home runs are always a big thrill,
especially for guys like me who don't hit
them that often. I wish I could figure out

(Eric Risberg, AP/Wide World Photos)

Our good buddy Kannon Kile surprised us with a visit to the dugout before Game 3 against the Giants. Here, Woody Williams and Andy Benes goof around with him. Kannon really helped us relax and must have been a good luck charm, since we won 5-4.

why you can do that on some days and on other days everything goes wrong. There are days when you are seeing the ball well—and I wish I could explain why that is—and there are other days when nothing feels right and you are just not going to get any hits.

I have gone so far as to write things down when things are going well—what I'm doing, what I'm thinking, my mechanics— trying to keep it going as long as I can. Every hitter is going to go through slumps at some points in the season. The only difference between good hitters and weak hitters is that the better a hitter is, the shorter the slump.

All through the postseason, for whatever reason, I felt good when I was at the plate. I had a good rhythm and was able to contribute some hits. It is always a good feeling to know you are helping the club.

That's what Kannon did for us today without realizing it. Late in the game, I came back to the bench after making a key out. He came up to me and asked if I wanted some of his peanut butter and jelly sandwich. I about fell off the bench because I was laughing so hard. Moments like that help you keep things in perspective. One thing this organization has been very good about is letting the kids hang around with their dads and be a part of everything. It is so nice to have them there.

*M. M.*

—— ANDY BENES

*I* think my attitude for the last several times I had pitched was that it could turn out to be my last game, so try to make it my best. I had that attitude when I pitched against Arizona and we clinched the first round of the playoffs, and that was the attitude I had going out to face the Giants in game four of the League Championship Series.

Even though we trailed in the series two games to one, I think I was the most relaxed I had ever been in any game in my life. My wife was with me on the trip, and that is always comforting. I really was surprised the good Lord had given me such a peace of mind, and I knew part of that also came from my wife.

I think another thing that helped me was having Kannon Kile there. He was such a big part of DK, and it was great having him right there in the dugout with us during those games in San Francisco. He was out running around on the field before the game, and it really brought home to me how baseball truly is a kid's game.

A big part of my decision to retire was my desire to be home with my kids. I don't want to miss more time at home. I want my kids to remember their dad being involved in their life and their activities. I had comfort in the fact that I knew I would have no regrets. I was leaving the game for the right reasons, and I was able to leave when I was really enjoying the game.

I got that feeling back when I was in Memphis on the rehab assignment in the summer. Having fun had not been part of the equation for a long time, and when my approach to the game changed and my attitude changed, it did start to become fun again.

I knew I was going to go out and pitch well, and with Matt [Morris] going the next day, everybody thought we were going to get the series back to St. Louis and win there and advance to the World Series.

We took a 2-0 lead in the first inning, and I was able to keep the Giants shut out, on two hits, into the sixth. I struck out the first hitter in the inning, then got two strikes on Jeff Kent. I was pitching him close, and I ended up walking him. Barry Bonds was coming up, and Dunc came out to the mound.

He told me to pitch him tough, which is basically saying you are going to walk him. We had the same strategy coming into the series as everybody does playing the Giants, which is that if somebody is going to beat us, it isn't going to be number 25. I had gotten him out the first two at-bats, but I did go ahead and walk him.

The Giants now had two guys on with one out and Benito Santiago coming up. I hadn't even looked at the bullpen; I was kind of oblivious to what was going on. Sometimes when Dunc comes to the mound, he will say, "This is going to be your last guy" or tell you what Tony is thinking, but I didn't get that impression when he came out before Bonds came up to bat. I had gotten Santiago out with inside fastballs both times up, and that's what I was thinking about when I saw Tony coming out to the mound.

I just thought, "Oh, man" because I knew unless we went to the World Series that this was going to be it. If I had known Bonds was going to be my last batter I might have pitched him a little differently. But it will always be kind of neat to say the last guy I faced in my career was Barry Bonds.

I had not given up any runs; we were ahead 2-0 and were 11 outs away from tying up the series. I walked off the mound with my head high, knowing I had done my job. I looked up to where my wife was sitting in the stands and gave her a smile.

Rick White had done such a good job for us that I still felt we were going to win, and he did strike out Santiago for the second out of the inning. J. T. Snow came up, however, and lined a two-run double that tied the game. It's always tough to watch when that happens, but the game was still tied 2-2 and it was now a three-inning game and I still thought we were going to win. There was no doubt in my mind.

It didn't turn out that way. The Giants won, and we were now a loss away from going home. I had a sense that my career was almost over.

I knew in my heart that it was the right time. It's much better to leave this game when things are going good than when they are going bad. It was time for my kids to be with their dad.

*A. B.*

—— JASON ISRINGHAUSEN

*A*ny time I get on the mound the game is on the line. I had a feeling today that if I did get into the game and we were winning, sometime during the ninth inning Barry Bonds would likely be coming up to bat.

My strategy was simple. I didn't want to have anybody on base in front of him. We were winning 5-4, so if Jeff Kent reached base ahead of Bonds, I would really be in a tough spot. Luckily, I was able to strike out Kent, which meant we could walk Bonds even though it meant putting the tying run on first. Everybody in the major leagues has the same game plan of not letting Barry Bonds beat you, but the whole key to that strategy working is that you have to be able to get the other guys out.

After walking Bonds, Benito Santiago was up and I was able to strike him out, too. That brought up Reggie Sanders, and we were able to get him to fly to right to end the game.

It was a game we had to win, and now we have to win tomorrow.

*J. J.*

———— JASON ISRINGHAUSEN

*I* really wanted to get into the game tonight, because our season was on the line. I knew the situation, however, and Tony was in a tough spot to figure out what to do. Matt pitched so well, but it didn't look like we were ever going to score. We went ahead 1-0 in the seventh, but the Giants tied it in the eighth.

Being a closer you have to understand that there are going to be games when you pitch when you don't want to and games when you don't pitch when you do want to. I probably could have gone two innings tonight, but we just were not in the right situation for that to happen.

Tony got the matchup he wanted, lefty vs. lefty, but Kenny Lofton was able to dunk a hit into right field off Steve Kline. They scored and won the game and the series. It was a real downer to watch the Giants celebrate and know we were going home and they were going to the World Series.

We know we should have won that series. We just left too many guys on base. We know that we could have played better and that we could be in the World Series. I don't know how we would have fared against the Angels, but I think we would have been all right. It's frustrating to know we should have beaten the Giants and that we had every opportunity to do it.

But that's baseball, and that's why we have next year. We wanted to go all the way for obvious reasons, but we always know that someone will be watching over us next year too. And we're going to be right after it again.

*J. J.*

—— MIKE MATHENY

*O*ur season ended tonight. We didn't think it would happen so soon, and it took some time after the game was over for it to sink in.

We knew we had to win to send the series back to St. Louis, and we were all confident. Matt [Morris] was really throwing well and we had a 1-0 lead going into the bottom of the eighth. Unfortunately, the Giants tied it that inning and scored another run in the ninth to win 2-1 and move on to the World Series.

The Giants had two outs and nobody on in the ninth when David Bell and Shawon Dunston singled. Tony decided to pull Matt and bring in Steve Kline. I never think back on pitching decisions. I don't let myself go there. The easiest thing in the world to do is second-guess a move that doesn't work out. People who make those decisions do it for a reason, and we made it as far as we did because of the decisions they made all year. I trust whoever we have out there.

Steve came in to face Lofton, runners on first and second, and he lined a single to right. I never know whether we are going to have a chance to get the guy at the plate or not. As soon as the ball is hit I try to size everything up. I take a peek at third to try to see where the runner is. I try to put all of those equations into play—how hard the ball is going to kick up off the grass and where we were playing Lofton. J. D. got to the ball quickly and got rid of it. I thought he might have a chance. He did everything he could, but the throw was just a little off-line.

(Ben Margot, AP/Wide World Photos)

*We pitched him tough, but Barry Bonds showed his versatility with a game-tying sacrifice fly in the eighth inning of Game 5. The Giants won by a final score of 2-1.*

This is the second year in a row we lost a playoff series on a play at the plate in the final inning. Steve was on the mound both times. I got both of those balls, and they weren't very happy endings.

It was a weird feeling. You don't want to get off the field because you don't want to give in yet. I think all of us really did believe we were going to win the game, come back to St. Louis, win the series and go on to the World Series. Matt pitched his heart out. He and I really had fun. It's hard to say that when you lose, but we actually did. In talking about it afterwards, I knew he had the same feelings I did. The intensity was so high, there were so many tough situations, and we were competing at the highest level with so much on the line. That's something you dream about when you are kids.

In those dreams, however, you are always on the winning team. We had plenty of chances; we just couldn't do anything, and that was so frustrating. In the series, we had just three hits in 39 chances with runners in scoring position. In our last two games, both one-run losses, we only had two hits in 25 opportunities with runners in scoring position. That is hard to explain.

When David Bell scored on Lofton's hit, you had to sit back and realize that was it. I sat on the bench for a while and kind of watched their celebration. There was a lot of jealousy, and then it sank in that it was over. That's playoff baseball. It can be over so quick.

As the Giants came off the bench to join the celebration on the field, one of their guys kind of forearmed Kline in the head. Steve started to go after him, so I grabbed him and told him that that wasn't the time. I told him we would deal with it later.

It was a very quiet and disappointed clubhouse. I give the Giants all the respect in the world because they beat us, but I don't think anybody in that room thought they were a better team than us. We knew we didn't play the way we wanted to play. Especially offensively, we knew we were a better team than we had shown. When it is over that quickly it is so hard to swallow. Unfortunately, we experienced that feeling two years in a row.

A lot of things go through your mind. It's hard to believe you are starting the off season, while they get to go on and have fun. All our bags were packed because we were coming back to St. Louis anyway. Most of the wives were there, and it was a quiet flight home.

It was really hard to believe it was our last game. We weren't ready for the season to end. It wasn't the time for reflection, because so much had happened. That would come later, when everybody involved knew it had truly been a special season.

*M. M.*

—— MATT MORRIS

*I*f I had timed my two games against the Giants differently the results of the series might have been different. Unfortunately that didn't happen, and when we lost tonight, it meant the end of our season.

I was determined to pitch better than I had in game one, mainly because I knew so much was at stake. Everybody in our locker room thought that if we could win this game and get the series back to St. Louis, we still had a great chance to win the series and go on to the World Series.

One thing I did differently was use a four-seam fastball. Dunc and I worked on it in the bullpen between my starts, so that I could have a pitch I could throw on the outer part of the plate to right-handed batters. I needed that pitch, especially in big situations, because my ball tends to run a little more, especially in intense moments, and I needed a pitch I could throw with confidence that would stay outside.

I went out there like I had thrown it all season and was able to get the Giants out. I threw the four-seamers mostly to right-handers, and because it was a different game plan, it worked. It's only a matter of spinning the ball. It's not really doing anything different, but it gets a different action than a two-seam fastball.

In games like this all I am trying to do is get outs and get us into the next inning. We had chances to score runs, but didn't.

It came down to the last inning. Tony has shown the last couple of years that he tends to stick with me in those situations, which I appreciate more than anything. It's a great sign that he has confidence in me. He could have taken me out earlier in the game, but I know I would really have been ticked off.

What happened tonight was I got two quick outs and was breezing through it, then I gave up hits on two first-pitch fastballs to two guys that I normally get out, David Bell and Shawon Dunston. That's why nobody was up in the bullpen. It wasn't like I fell behind in the count; it was just boom, boom, and two guys were on.

Bell has picked it up a little bit, but I should have known Dunston would be ready for that pitch. I got outsmarted by both of them because both pitches were not that bad. In the regular season they don't swing at those pitches, but in the playoffs when the game is on the line, they do the little things.

(Julie Jacobson, AP/Wide World Photos)

We stare in disappointment from the dugout as we realize that our season is over with one swing of Kenny Lofton's bat. With his two-out *RBI* single, the Giants clinched the *NLCS* and will go to the World Series. As discouraging as losing in the postseason is, we are proud to have made it this far, especially considering all the reasons we had to give up.

You tend to think about situations more, and you play a different game. Guys are bunting, not caring if they are giving themselves up, knowing the team is struggling to score runs. It boggles my mind that during the season those approaches aren't taken all the time. You're still playing for the same thing. When you are trying to win a ballgame, all of the little things come into play.

I left the game and Steve Kline came in. He battles all the time, but it was over in a heartbeat for him, too. We went from having a chance to win to losing the game in less than 10 minutes, and the most time was spent watching Kline warm up.

I sat on the bench for I don't know how long—it felt like forever—but I don't think it was that long. It was tough to see the Giants celebrating, running around on the field and going crazy. Another DK line was, "You're only as good as your last game." Tonight our last game wasn't good enough.

Everybody wants to win every year, but this year we had different reasons why we wanted to win—unfortunate reasons—but it wasn't meant to be.

Next year we are going to have the same goal, but hopefully we will have more positives to go off of, and hopefully our last game we will be good enough. One thing won't change. We will still be doing it for DK.

*M. M.*

# PLAYER CAPSULES

## —ANDY BENES

He enjoyed one of the most remarkable
seasons in the major leagues in 2002. After
three disappointing starts in April, going 0-2
with a 10.80 ERA, Andy left the Cardinals,
and most people thought his career was over.
He returned in July, however, and proceeded
to post a 1.86 ERA for the rest of the season,
the best mark in the major leagues. In his
final 14 starts of the season over that stretch,
he went 5-2, and only once did he allow
three runs in a game. After the season, Andy
announced that he was retiring for good.

## —MIGUEL CAIRO

A valuable reserve during the regular season,
Miguel came off the bench to fill in for the
injured Scott Rolen in the playoffs. His 16
hits in the regular season ranked second
among pinch hitters, his .322 average was fifth

among pinch hitters, and he tied for third in pinch RBIs with 16. Miguel started games at first base, second base, shortstop, third base, left field and designated hitter. He joined the Cardinals after being claimed on waivers from the Cubs in 2001.

# —MIKE CRUDALE

The rookie right-hander enjoyed a productive season after being recalled from Triple A Memphis. He appeared in 49 games, going 3-0 with a 1.88 ERA. All but one of his appearances were in middle relief; he made an emergency start against the Expos on April 27 and pitched two scoreless innings. Mike was originally selected by the Cardinals in the 24th round of the 1999 draft.

# —MIKE DIFELICE

This veteran was signed as a free agent to be a backup to catcher Mike Matheny and contributed several key hits during the season.

He opened the year with a bang, hitting a home run on Opening Day in the win against Colorado. He was the usual catcher for Matt Morris and was the starting catcher for four of the Cardinals' eight shutouts during the season.

## —J. D. DREW

The Cardinals' regular right fielder battled through an injury-plagued season that limited his offensive production and forced him to undergo knee surgery following the end of the year. He was limited to 135 games and saw his average drop from .323 in 2001 to .252, his home run total drop from 27 to 18, and his RBI total drop from 73 to 56. He still excelled defensively. In one game at Houston on September 13, he took a home run away from Jeff Bagwell with a leaping catch and in the same inning threw out Craig Biggio at the plate. He had a key home run off Curt Schilling of the Diamondbacks in the final week of the season. Drew was originally selected by the Cardinals in the first round of the 1998 draft.

## —JIM EDMONDS

He turned in his third consecutive outstanding season with the Cardinals in 2002, both offensively and defensively. He hit a career-high .311 with 28 homers and 83 RBIs and showed his skills in the outfield, winning another Gold Glove and leading the team with 11 outfield assists. Seven of his 28 homers came against the division-rival Astros. He spent two weeks on the disabled list in June with a sore right wrist. Edmonds was acquired by the Cardinals from Anaheim in a spring training trade in 2000 for second baseman Adam Kennedy and pitcher Kent Bottenfield.

# —JEFF FASSERO

He was acquired by the Cardinals in a trade from the Chicago Cubs on August 25, 2002 for two minor-league pitchers, joining the team in time for the stretch run and the playoffs. He was teamed with Steve Kline to give the Cardinals two quality setup left-handed relievers in front of closer Jason Isringhausen. He earned three victories in 16 appearances. Jeff spent six years in the Cardinals' farm system from 1984-89, but was never promoted to the major-league roster.

# —CHUCK FINLEY

He proved to be a valuable addition to the Cardinals' starting rotation after he was acquired in a trade from Cleveland on July 19, 2002 in exchange for two minor-leaguers. He went 7-4 in 14 starts for the Cardinals, with his final win of the year on September 28, earning Chuck his 200<sup>th</sup> career victory. He ranks 19<sup>th</sup> all-time with 2,610 career strikeouts. One of his unnoticed contributions to the team was helping teach Andy Benes the split-finger fastball that was so important to his success in the second half of the year.

## —JASON ISRINGHAUSEN

He was signed by the Cardinals as a free agent from Oakland to take over the closer's role in the bullpen. A native of nearby Brighton, Illinois, his homecoming was successful, as he saved 32 games in 37 opportunities. He suffered from a sore right shoulder for much of the season, which eventually required surgery. He enjoyed a terrific month of May, when he saved 12 games, the highest one-month total of his career, tying the major-league record for most saves in the month of May. Isringhausen also went into the

record book on April 13 by striking out the
side against Houston on nine pitches.

## —STEVE KLINE

He was a busy reliever again in 2002, appear-
ing in 66 games, which actually was a drop
from his league-leading totals of the three
previous seasons. He missed the entire month
of May while on the disabled list with a
strained arm. He earned six saves to go along
with his two victories. He was known almost
as well for his trademark dirty cap as he was
for his success on the mound. Steve joined
the Cardinals before the 2001 season in a
trade with the Montreal Expos.

## —ELI MARRERO

He had the best season of his brief major-
league career in 2002, as he moved out from
behind the plate to log more playing time in

the outfield. He posted career highs in nearly every offensive category, as he hit .262 with 18 homers and 66 RBIs, filling in frequently for the injured J. D. Drew and Jim Edmonds. He also stole 14 bases and was thrown out only three times. Eli was originally selected by the Cardinals in the 1993 draft and made the majors in 1997 after five years in the minors.

## —TINO MARTINEZ

He was signed by the Cardinals as a free agent from the New York Yankees and was expected to add veteran leadership to the team as he took the place of the retired Mark McGwire at first base. He suffered a disappointing year offensively as he struggled to make the adjustment to National League pitching. He did finish the year with 21 homers and 75 RBIs while hitting .262, 11 percentage points below his career average. He earned a spot in the postseason for the eighth consecutive year, one previously with Seattle and six with the Yankees.

## —MIKE MATHENY

He enjoyed another outstanding defensive season in 2002, as he committed only four errors in 106 games and threw out 34 percent of opposing base stealers. Only 65 runners even attempted to steal on Mike because of his throwing ability. He raised his batting average 26 points to .244 after a dedicated off-season workout program. Matheny was signed by the Cardinals as a free agent from Toronto after the 1999 season.

## —MATT MORRIS

He was once again the ace of the Cardinals' staff, winning 17 games and ranking among the best starters in the league. He was selected for the All-Star team, but did not pitch. He improved his combined record for the past two years to 39-17 and raised his career record at Busch Stadium to 36-18. He missed three starts when he was on the disabled list in August and September because of a strained hamstring. Matt was originally selected by the Cardinals in the first round of the 1995 draft.

## —EDUARDO PEREZ

He proved that he could provide power coming off the bench, as he hit 10 homers in just 154 at-bats. Three of his homers came as a pinch hitter, and he also drove in 10 runs as a pinch hitter, the third highest total in the NL. He started games in right field, left field, at first base and designated hitter in his reserve role. Perez signed with the Cardinals as a minor-league free agent before the 2002 season and made the team in spring training.

# —ALBERT PUJOLS

He had another record-breaking year in his second year with the Cardinals, picking up where his 2001 Rookie of the Year season ended. He finished second to the Giants' Barry Bonds in MVP voting after hitting .314 with 34 homers, 127 RBIs and 118 runs scored, all team highs. He became the first player in major-league history to hit .300 with 30 homers, 100 RBIs and 100 runs scored in each of his first two seasons in the majors. He became only the fifth Cardinal in history to hit 30 or more homers in consecutive seasons, and he was the first to hit 20 or more homers in his first two seasons. Pujols was originally selected by the Cardinals in the 10th round of the 1999 draft and made the majors after playing only 133 games in the minors.

# —EDGAR RENTERIA

He earned both a Silver Slugger and Gold Glove for his outstanding offensive and defensive performance in 2002. He enjoyed his best offensive season to date, hitting .305 with 11 homers and 83 RBIs, tying the team record for most RBIs for a shortstop, which had stood since 1921. He had the third highest average (.372) in the NL with runners in scoring position. He provided perhaps the single biggest hit of the season with his three-run walk-off homer against the Cubs on July 28, capping a six-run ninth-inning rally that gave the Cardinals a 10-9 victory. Renteria was acquired by the Cardinals prior to the 1999 season in a trade with the Florida Marlins.

# —Kerry Robinson

A St. Louis native, he spent his first full season in the major leagues as a reserve outfielder. He contributed 13 pinch hits and also started games in all three outfield positions. He played in a career-high 124 games. Robinson was originally selected by the Cardinals in the 34th round of the 1995 draft, was selected by Tampa Bay in the expansion draft in 1997, and rejoined the Cardinals as a minor-league free agent prior to the 2001 season.

# —Scott Rolen

He joined the Cardinals in a trade with the Philadelphia Phillies on July 29, 2002 in exchange for pitchers Bud Smith and Mike Timlin and infielder Placido Polanco. He proved to be a great addition over the final two months of the season, hitting 14 homers and driving in 44 runs as a Cardinal while hitting .278. He earned Silver Slugger and Gold Glove award for his combined success with the Phillies and Cardinals, 31 homers and 110 RBIs. He signed an eight-year contract extension, tying him to the Cardinals through 2010.

## —JASON SIMONTACCHI

He came out of virtual anonymity to become a solid starter for the Cardinals, winning his first five games and finishing with 11 victories, second on the staff. A 28-year veteran of six minor-league seasons, Jason had pitched in independent baseball and in Italy as well as for the Royals, Pirates and Twins organizations. He was signed by the Cardinals as a minor-league free agent prior to the 2002 season. He was named the NL Rookie of the Month for June when he went 3-1 to raise his record at the time to 6-1.

# —GARRETT STEPHENSON

He spent much of the 2002 season on the disabled list as he began his comeback from elbow surgery in 2001. He was limited to just 12 games and 10 starts because of shoulder tightness and an injury to his hamstring, which required surgery. Garrett was acquired by the Cardinals in a trade with the Phillies prior to the 1999 season.

# —DAVE VERES

He relinquished the closer role to Jason Isringhausen, but turned in a quality perfor-mance as a setup reliever. He led the staff in holds and appearances while also picking up three wins and four saves. Veres was acquired by the Cardinals prior to the 2000 season in a trade with the Colorado Rockies.

## —FERNANDO VINA

He had a slight dropoff in his offensive performance from 2001, but still excelled defensively, winning his second consecutive Gold
Glove. He proved to be a very effective run
producer out of the leadoff spot, driving in
54 runs, the most by a leadoff hitter in the
NL. He struck out just 36 times in 622 at-bats
and was the catalyst in the playoff victory
over Arizona. Vina joined the Cardinals prior
to the 2000 season in a trade from the Milwaukee Brewers.

## —RICK WHITE

He was signed by the Cardinals as a minor-
league free agent on August 17, 2002 after he
had been released by Colorado. He joined the
Cardinals after a week at Triple A Memphis
and became a quality member of the bullpen,
going 3-1 with an ERA of 0.82 in 20 appear-

ances. White allowed only 13 hits in 22 innings, allowing only two earned runs.

# —WOODY WILLIAMS

He missed much of the season because of injuries, but was very effective when he did pitch, going 9-4 in his 17 starts. The Cardinals scored a combined four runs in Woody's four losses. In his less than two seasons as a Cardinal, Williams's career record is 16-5, and the Cardinals went 20-8 in the games he started. He was acquired from San Diego in a trade for Ray Lankford on August 2, 2001.

| Date | Team | Score | Winner-Loser-Save | W-L | STD | GA/GB |
|---|---|---|---|---|---|---|
| 4/1 | COL | W, 10-2 | Morris-Hampton-None | 1-0 | T1 | — |
| 4/2 | | | OPEN DATE | | T1 | — |
| 4/3 | COL | L, 6-3 | Neagle-Stephenson-Jimenez | 1-1 | T1 | — |
| 4/4 | COL | L, 6-1 | Thomson-Benes-None | 1-2 | T4 | -1.0 |
| 4/5 | @HOU | W, 5-1 | Stechschulte-Micki-None | 2-2 | T2 | -1.0 |
| 4/6 | @HOU | W, 8-4 | Morris-Cruz-None | 3-2 | 2 | -1.0 |
| 4/7 | @HOU | L, 7-6 (12) | Stone-Hackman-None | 3-3 | T2 | -1.5 |
| 4/8 | | | OPEN DATE | | 3 | -2.0 |
| 4/9 | MIL | W, 6-5 | Veres-Cabrera-Isringhausen | 4-3 | 2 | -1.5 |
| 4/10 | MIL | W, 6-5 (11) | Isringhausen-Vizcaino-None | 5-3 | 2 | -0.5 |
| 4/11 | MIL | W, 6-5 | Veres-Cabrera-Kline | 6-3 | 1 | +0.5 |
| 4/12 | HOU | W, 7-3 | Morris-Miller-None | 7-3 | 1 | +1.0 |
| 4/13 | HOU | W, 2-1 | Isringhausen-Stone-None | 8-3 | 1 | +1.0 |
| 4/14 | HOU | L, 5-4 | Renolds-Stephenson-Wagner | 8-4 | 1 | +1.0 |
| 4/15 | @ARI | L, 14-5 | Helling-Benes-None | 8-5 | 1 | +0.5 |
| 4/16 | @ARI | L, 5-3 | Johnson-B. Smith-Myers | 8-6 | 2 | -0.5 |
| 4/17 | @ARI | W, 8-4 | Morris-Schilling-Isringhausen | 9-6 | 2 | -0.5 |
| 4/18 | @MIL | L, 7-5 | Cabrera-Hackman-DeJean | 9-7 | 2 | -1.0 |
| 4/19 | @MIL | L, 6-1 | Quevedo-Timlin-Vizcaino | 9-8 | 2 | -2.0 |
| 4/20 | @MIL | L, 5-3 | Vizcaino-Veres-DeJean | 9-9 | 3 | -3.0 |
| 4/21 | @MIL | L, 5-3 | Neugebauer-B. Smith-DeJean | 9-10 | 3 | -4.0 |
| 4/22 | | | OPEN DATE | | 3 | -4.0 |
| 4/23 | @NY | L, 4-3 | D'Amico-Morris-Benitez | 9-11 | 3 | -4.0 |
| 4/24 | @NY | W, 4-2 | Kile-Leiter-Isringhausen | 10-11 | 3 | -3.0 |
| 4/25 | @NY | L, 7-6 | Strickland-Veres-Benitez | 10-12 | 3 | -4.0 |
| 4/26 | @MON | W, 7-6 (11) | Stechschulte-Ohka-Veres | 11-12 | 3 | -3.5 |
| 4/27 | @MON | W, 5-0 | Matthews-Chen-None | 12-12 | 3 | -3.5 |
| 4/28 | @MON | L, 5-2 | Ohka-Morris-Herges | 12-13 | 3 | -3.5 |
| 4/29 | | | OPEN DATE | | 3 | -3.5 |
| 4/30 | FLA | L, 7-2 | Burnett-Kile-None | 12-14 | 3 | -4.5 |

| Date | Team | Score | Winner-Loser-Save | W-L | STD | GA/GB |
|------|------|-------|-------------------|-----|-----|-------|
| 5/1 | FLA | W, 6-4 | T. Smith-Dempster-Isringhausen | 13-14 | 3 | -4.5 |
| 5/2 | FLA | L, 9-6 | Tejera-Veres-Nunez | 13-15 | 3 | -4.5 |
| 5/3 | ATL | L, 2-1 (11) | Hammond- Stechschulte-Smoltz | 13-16 | 3 | -4.5 |
| 5/4 | ATL | W, 3-2 | Simontacchi-Lopez-Isringhausen | 14-16 | 3 | -3.5 |
| 5/5 | ATL | L, 4-2 | Maddux-Kile-Smoltz | 14-17 | 4 | -3.5 |
| 5/6 | @CHI | L, 6-5 | Fassero-Timlin-None | 14-18 | 4 | -4.5 |
| 5/7 | @CHI | L, 8-0 | WOOD-B. Smith-None | 14-19 | T4 | -5.5 |
| 5/8 | @CHI | W, 3-2 | Morris-Cruz-Isringhausen | 15-19 | T3 | -5.5 |
| 5/9 | | | OPEN DATE | | | -5.5 |
| 5/10 | @CIN | W, 4-2 | Stechschulte-G. White-Isringhausen | 16-19 | 3 | -4.5 |
| 5/11 | @CIN | L, 8-1 | Reitsma-Kile-None | 16-20 | 3 | -5.5 |
| 5/12 | @CIN | W, 10-8 | Stechschulte-Graves-Isringhausen | 17-20 | 3 | -4.5 |
| 5/13 | CHI | W, 3-0 | MORRIS-Wood-None | 18-20 | 3 | -4.5 |
| 5/14 | CHI | W, 11-2 | Timlin-Cruz-None | 19-20 | 3 | -4.5 |
| 5/15 | CHI | W, 4-1 | Stechschulte-Bere-Isringhausen | 20-20 | T2 | -4.5 |
| 5/16 | | | OPEN DATE | | | -5.0 |
| 5/17 | CIN | W, 3-1 | Kile-Sullivan-Isringhausen | 21-20 | 2 | -4.0 |
| 5/18 | CIN | L, 7-3 | Rijo-Morris-None | 21-21 | T2 | -5.0 |
| 5/19 | CIN | W, 10-1 | Stephenson-Acevedo-None | 22-21 | 2 | -4.0 |
| 5/20 | CIN | W, 7-3 | Williams-Haynes-None | 23-21 | 2 | -3.0 |
| 5/21 | HOU | W, 3-1 | Simontacchi-Hernandez-Isringhausen | 24-21 | 2 | -3.0 |
| 5/22 | HOU | W, 3-2 | Veres-Stone-None | 25-21 | 2 | -3.0 |
| 5/23 | HOU | W, 5-4 | Hackman-Dotel-Isringhausen | 26-21 | 2 | -2.0 |
| 5/24 | @PIT | L, 5-2 | Wells-Stephenson-None | 26-22 | 2 | -2.0 |
| 5/25 | @PIT | W, 6-3 | Williams-Anderson-Isringhausen | 27-22 | 2 | -2.0 |
| 5/26 | @PIT | W, 7-3 | Simontacchi-Fogg-None | 28-22 | 2 | -1.0 |
| 5/27 | @HOU | W, 4-3 | Simontacchi-Oswalt-Isringhausen | 29-22 | 2 | -0.5 |
| 5/28 | @HOU | W, 4-1 | Morris-Reynolds-Isringhausen | 30-22 | 2 | -0.5 |
| 5/29 | @HOU | L, 10-5 | Redding-Stephenson-None | 30-23 | 2 | -1.5 |
| 5/30 | | | OPEN DATE | | | -2.0 |
| 5/31 | PIT | L, 3-1 | Fogg-Williams-M. Williams | 30-24 | 2 | -2.0 |

| Date | Team | Score | Winner-Loser-Save | W-L | STD | GA/GB |
|---|---|---|---|---|---|---|
| 6/1 | PIT | W, 9-4 | Kile-Arroyo-None | 31-24 | 2 | -1.0 |
| 6/2 | PIT | L, 5-2 | Lowe-Morris-Williams | 31-25 | 2 | -2.0 |
| 6/3 | | | | OPEN DATE | | 2 | -2.0 |
| 6/4 | @CIN | W, 8-5 | Simontacchi-Hamilton-None | 32-25 | 2 | -1.0 |
| 6/5 | @CIN | | PPD-RAIN | | 2 | -1.0 |
| 6/6 | @CIN | L, 3-2 | Haynes-Williams-Graves | 32-26 | 2 | -2.0 |
| 6/7 | @KC | W, 12-6 | Kile-Byrd-None | 33-26 | 2 | -1.0 |
| 6/8 | @KC | W, 11-3 | Morris-Affeldt-None | 34-26 | 2 | -1.0 |
| 6/9 | @KC | L, 3-2 | Hernandez-Timlin-None | 34-27 | 2 | -1.0 |
| 6/10 | @SEA | L, 10-0 | MOYER-B. Smith-None | 34-28 | 2 | -1.0 |
| 6/11 | @SEA | W, 7-4 | Williams-Baldwin-None | 35-28 | 2 | -1.0 |
| 6/12 | @SEA | L, 5-0 | PINEIRO-Kile-None | 35-29 | 2 | -1.0 |
| 6/13 | | | OPEN DATE | | 2 | -1.0 |
| 6/14 | KC | W, 3-0 | Morris-Asencio-Kline | 36-29 | 1 | -1.0 |
| 6/15 | KC | W, 5-3 | Simontacchi-Suppan-Veres | 37-29 | 2 | -1.0 |
| 6/16 | KC | W, 5-1 | WILLIAMS-May-None | 38-29 | T1 | — |
| 6/17 | | | OPEN DATE | | T1 | — |
| 6/18 | ANA | W, 7-2 | Kile-Appier-None | 39-29 | 1 | +1.0 |
| 6/19 | ANA | W, 6-2 | Morris-Sele-None | 40-29 | 1 | +2.0 |
| 6/20 | ANA | L, 3-2 | Schoeneweis-B. Smith-Percival | 40-30 | 1 | +2.0 |
| 6/21 | @CHI | L, 2-1 | LEIBER-Williams-None | 40-31 | 1 | +2.0 |
| 6/22 | @CHI | | PPD-DARRYL KILE DEATH | | 1 | +2.5 |
| 6/23 | @CHI | L, 8-3 | Wood-Simontacchi-None | 40-32 | 1 | +2.5 |
| 6/24 | | | OPEN DATE | | 1 | +3.0 |
| 6/25 | MIL | L, 2-0 | RUSCH-Morris-None | 40-33 | 1 | +2.0 |
| 6/26 | MIL | W, 5-2 | Williams-Wright-Isringhausen | 41-33 | 1 | +2.0 |
| 6/27 | MIL | L, 7-2 (11) | Vizcaino-Stechschulte-None | 41-34 | 1 | +1.0 |
| 6/28 | CIN | W, 3-2 | Simontacchi-Reitsma-Isringhausen | 42-34 | 1 | +2.0 |
| 6/29 | CIN | L, 4-2 | Dessens-Hackman-Graves | 42-35 | 1 | +1.0 |
| 6/30 | CIN | L, 12-8 | Sullivan-Isringhausen-None | 42-36 | T1 | — |

| Date | Team | Score | Winner-Loser-Save | W-L | STD | GA/GB |
|------|------|-------|-------------------|-----|-----|-------|
| 7/1 | SD | W, 7-3 | Williams-O. Perez-None | 43-36 | T1 | — |
| 7/2 | SD | W, 11-5 | Crudale-Jarvis-None | 44-36 | 1 | +1.0 |
| 7/3 | SD | W, 4-1 | Simontacchi-Lawrence-Isringhausen | 45-36 | 1 | +2.0 |
| 7/4 | LA | W, 3-2 | T. Smith-Ishii-Isringhausen | 46-36 | 1 | +3.0 |
| 7/5 | LA | L, 6-5 | O. Perez-Morris-Gagne | 46-37 | 1 | +2.0 |
| 7/6 | LA | L, 4-2 (11) | Quantrill-Kline-Gagne | 46-38 | 1 | +1.0 |
| 7/7 | LA | W, 12-6 | Matthews-Daal-None | 47-38 | 1 | +2.0 |
| 7/8 | | | ALL-STAR BREAK | | 1 | +2.0 |
| 7/9 | | | ALL-STAR GAME | | 1 | +2.0 |
| 7/10 | | | ALL-STAR BREAK | | 1 | +2.0 |
| 7/11 | | | OPEN DATE | | 1 | +2.5 |
| 7/12 | @SD | L, 4-3 | Holtz-Veres-Hoffman | 47-39 | 1 | +2.5 |
| 7/13 | @SD | W, 2-1 (10) | Crudale-Reed-Isringhausen | 48-39 | 1 | +3.5 |
| 7/14 | @SD | W, 4-1 | B. Smith-B. Jones-Isringhausen | 49-39 | 1 | +3.5 |
| 7/15 | @LA | W, 4-2 | T. Smith-Daal-Isringhausen | 50-39 | 1 | +3.5 |
| 7/16 | @LA | W, 9-2 | Hackman-Nomo-None | 51-39 | 1 | +3.5 |
| 7/17 | SF | L, 5-4 | Worrell-Veres-Nen | 51-40 | 1 | +3.5 |
| 7/18 | SF | W, 5-1 | Morris-Schmidt-None | 52-40 | 1 | +3.5 |
| 7/19 | @PIT | L, 12-9 | Sauerbeck-Veres-None | 52-41 | 1 | +3.5 |
| 7/20 | @PIT | L, 15-6 | Benson-T. Smith-None | 52-42 | 1 | +3.5 |
| 7/21 | @PIT | W, 8-4 | Finley-Fogg-Kline | 53-42 | 1 | +3.5 |
| 7/22 | @SF | W, 5-3 | Hackman-Worrell-Isringhausen | 54-42 | 1 | +4.5 |
| 7/23 | @SF | W, 4-0 | Morris-Schmidt-None | 55-42 | 1 | +4.5 |
| 7/24 | @SF | L, 6-4 | Rueter-Benes-Nen | 55-43 | 1 | +3.5 |
| 7/25 | @SF | W, 4-3 | T. Smith-Jensen-Isringhausen | 56-43 | 1 | +4.0 |
| 7/26 | CHI | W, 8-4 | Finley-Lieber-None | 57-43 | 1 | +5.0 |
| 7/27 | CHI | L, 7-3 | Wood-Simontacchi-None | 57-44 | 1 | +4.0 |
| 7/28 | CHI | W, 10-9 | Veres-Alfonseca-None | 58-44 | 1 | +5.0 |
| 7/29 | | | OPEN DATE | | 1 | +5.0 |
| 7/30 | @FLA | W, 5-0 | Benes-Tejera-None | 59-44 | 1 | +5.0 |
| 7/31 | @FLA | L, 8-5 | Beckett-T. Smith-Looper | 59-45 | 1 | +5.0 |

| Date | Team | Score | Winner-Loser-Save | W-L | STD | GA/GB |
|------|------|-------|-------------------|-----|-----|-------|
| 8/1 | @FLA | L, 4-0 | BURNETT-Finley-None | 59-46 | 1 | +4.0 |
| 8/2 | @ATL | L, 11-5 | Glavine-Simontacchi-None | 59-47 | 1 | +4.0 |
| 8/3 | @ATL | L, 6-1 | Marquis-Morris-None | 59-48 | 1 | +3.0 |
| 8/4 | @ATL | L, 2-1 | Smoltz-Veres-None | 59-49 | 1 | +2.0 |
| 8/5 | | | OPEN DATE | | | +2.0 |
| 8/6 | MON | L, 10-1 | YOSHII-Finley-None | 59-50 | 1 | +2.0 |
| 8/6 | MON | L, 4-1 | Ohka-Simontacchi-Stewart | 59-51 | 1 | +1.0 |
| 8/8 | MON | W, 5-3 | Morris-Reames-Isringhausen | 60-51 | 1 | +2.0 |
| 8/9 | NY | L, 2-1 | Leiter-Matthews-Benitez | 60-52 | 1 | +2.0 |
| 8/10 | NY | W, 5-4 | Veres-Reed-Isringhausen | 61-52 | 1 | +2.0 |
| 8/11 | NY | W, 9-0 | Finley-Astacio-None | 62-52 | 1 | +2.0 |
| 8/12 | @PIT | W, 10-6 | Simontacchi-Meadows-None | 63-52 | 1 | +2.5 |
| 8/13 | @PIT | W, 9-5 | Morris-Anderson-Isringhausen | 64-52 | 1 | +3.0 |
| 8/14 | @PIT | W, 7-3 | Benes-Wells-None | 65-52 | 1 | +3.0 |
| 8/15 | @PIT | W, 11-5 | Kline-Williams-None | 66-52 | 1 | +4.0 |
| 8/16 | @PHI | L, 4-0 | WOLF-Finley-None | 66-53 | 1 | +4.0 |
| 8/17 | @PHI | W, 5-1 | Simontacchi-Coggin-None | 67-53 | 1 | +4.0 |
| 8/18 | @PHI | W, 5-1 | Morris-Padilla-None | 68-53 | 1 | +5.0 |
| 8/19 | PIT | W, 7-2 | Benes-Wells-None | 69-53 | 1 | +5.0 |
| 8/20 | PIT | L, 8-0 | Benson-Hackman-None | 69-54 | 1 | +5.0 |
| 8/21 | PIT | W, 4-1 | Finley-Fogg-Isringhausen | 70-54 | 1 | +5.0 |
| 8/22 | PIT | W, 5-4 | Molina-Williams-None | 71-54 | 1 | +5.0 |
| 8/23 | PHI | L, 5-4 (14) | Adams-Joseph-None | 71-55 | 1 | +4.0 |
| 8/24 | PHI | L, 4-0 | Padilla-Benes-Mesa | 71-56 | 1 | +4.0 |
| 8/25 | PHI | L, 5-3 | Silva-Isringhausen-Mesa | 71-57 | 1 | +3.0 |
| 8/26 | | | OPEN DATE | | | +3.0 |
| 8/27 | @CIN | L, 5-4 | Reitsma-Simontacchi-Graves | 71-58 | 1 | +2.5 |
| DH | @CIN | W, 5-0 | FINLEY-Dessens-None | 72-58 | 1 | +3.5 |
| 8/28 | @CIN | W, 9-2 | Kline-Estes-None | 73-58 | 1 | +3.5 |
| 8/29 | @CIN | L, 7-0 | Haynes-Williams-None | 73-59 | 1 | +2.5 |
| 8/30 | @CHI | W, 6-3 | Wright-Zambrano-Veres | 74-59 | 1 | +2.5 |
| 8/31 | @CHI | W, 8-1 | Hackman-Prior-None | 75-59 | 1 | +3.0 |
| DH | @CHI | W, 10-4 | Benes-Bere-None | 76-59 | 1 | +4.0 |

| Date | Team | Score | Winner-Loser-Save | W-L | STD | GA/GB |
|---|---|---|---|---|---|---|
| 9/1 | @CHI | L, 5-4 | Cruz-Finley-Alfonseca | 76-60 | 1 | +4.0 |
| 9/2 | CIN | L, 5-3 | Estes-Stephenson-Graves | 76-61 | 1 | +4.0 |
| 9/3 | CIN | W, 3-1 | Williams-Haynes-Veres | 77-61 | 1 | +4.0 |
| 9/4 | CIN | W, 10-5 | Hackman-Chen-None | 78-61 | 1 | +5.0 |
| 9/5 | | | OPEN DATE | | 1 | +4.5 |
| 9/6 | CHI | W, 11-2 | AN. BENES-Al. Benes-None | 79-61 | 1 | +5.5 |
| 9/7 | CHI | W, 6-5 (13) | Fassero-Alfonseca-None | 80-61 | 1 | +5.5 |
| 9/8 | CHI | W, 3-1 | Simontacchi-Wood-Kline | 81-61 | 1 | +5.5 |
| 9/9 | @MIL | W, 3-0 | Williams-Diggins-Kline | 82-61 | 1 | +5.5 |
| 9/10 | @MIL | W, 8-3 | Morris-Franklin-None | 83-61 | 1 | +6.5 |
| 9/11 | @MIL | W, 4-3 | Fassero-Sheets-Isringhausen | 84-61 | 1 | +5.5 |
| 9/12 | @HOU | L, 6-3 | Dotel-Veres-Wagner | 84-62 | 1 | +6.5 |
| 9/13 | @HOU | W, 3-2 (10) | White-Gordon-Isringhausen | 85-62 | 1 | +7.5 |
| 9/14 | @HOU | W, 2-1 | Williams-Munro-Isringhausen | 86-62 | 1 | +6.5 |
| 9/15 | @HOU | L, 8-0 | MILLER-Morris-None | 86-63 | 1 | +6.5 |
| 9/16 | | | OPEN DATE | | | |
| 9/17 | @COL | W, 11-4 | Fassero-Mercker-None | 87-63 | 1 | +7.5 |
| 9/18 | @COL | W, 8-5 | White-Speier-Kline | 88-63 | 1 | +7.5 |
| 9/19 | @COL | W, 12-6 | Simontacchi-Jennings-None | 89-63 | 1 | +8.5 |
| 9/20 | HOU | W, 9-3 | White-Munro-None | 90-63 | 1 | +9.5 |
| 9/21 | HOU | L, 6-3 | Miller-Morris-None | 90-64 | 1 | +8.5 |
| 9/22 | HOU | W, 7-3 | Finley-Saarloos-None | 91-64 | 1 | +9.5 |
| 9/23 | ARI | W, 13-1 | Wright-Helling-None | 92-64 | 1 | +9.5 |
| 9/24 | ARI | W, 3-2 | Isringhausen-Fetters-None | 93-64 | 1 | +10.5 |
| 9/25 | ARI | W, 6-1 | Stephenson-Schilling-None | 94-64 | 1 | +10.5 |
| 9/26 | MIL | W, 9-1 | Morris-Diggins-None | 95-64 | 1 | +11.0 |
| 9/27 | MIL | L, 2-1 | Sheets-White-DeJean | 95-65 | 1 | +11.0 |
| 9/28 | MIL | W, 3-1 | Finley-Rusch-Isringhausen | 96-65 | 1 | +12.0 |
| 9/29 | MIL | W, 4-0 | Crudale-Vizcaino-None | 97-65 | 1 | +13.0 |

## National League Division Series

| | | | | |
|---|---|---|---|---|
| 10/1 | @ARI | W, 12-2 | Morris-Johnson-None | 1-0 |
| 10/3 | @ARI | W, 2-1 | Fassero-Koplove-Isringhausen | 2-0 |
| 10/5 | ARI | W, 6-3 | Fassero-Batista-None | 3-0 |

## National League Championship Series

| | | | | |
|---|---|---|---|---|
| 10/9 | SF | L, 9-6 | Rueter-Morris-Nen | 0-1 |
| 10/10 | SF | L, 4-1 | Schmidt-Williams-Nen | 0-2 |
| 10/12 | @SF | W, 5-4 | Finley-Witasick-Isringhausen | 1-2 |
| 10/13 | @SF | L, 4-3 | Worrell-White-Nen | 1-3 |
| 10/14 | @SF | L, 2-1 | Worrell-Morris-None | 1-4 |

Note: Complete games in CAPS

# National League Departmental Leaders

## Batting Average

| | | |
|---|---|---|
| .370 | Bonds, B | SF |
| .338 | Walker, L | COL |
| .336 | Guerrero, V | MON |
| .329 | Helton, T | COL |
| .327 | Jones, C | ATL |
| .315 | Vidro, J | MON |
| **.314** | **Pujols, A** | **STL** |
| .313 | Kent, J | SF |
| **.311** | **Edmonds, J** | **STL** |
| .308 | Alfonzo, E | NY |

## Runs

| | | |
|---|---|---|
| 122 | Sosa,S | CHI |
| **118** | **Pujols, A** | **STL** |
| 117 | Bonds, B | SF |
| 110 | Green, S. | LA |
| 107 | Helton, T | COL |
| 106 | Berkman, L | HOU |
| 103 | Spivey Jr., J | ARI |
| 103 | Vidro, J | MON |

## Hits

| | | |
|---|---|---|
| 206 | Guerrero, V | MON |
| 195 | Kent, J | SF |
| 190 | Vidro, J | MON |
| **185** | **Pujols, A** | **STL** |
| 185 | Castillo, L | FLA |
| 183 | Walker, T | CIN |
| 182 | Helton, T | COL |
| 179 | Jones, C | ATL |
| 176 | Abreu, B | PHI |
| 175 | Furcal, R | ATL |

## Doubles

| | | |
|---|---|---|
| 50 | Abreu, B | PHI |
| 44 | Lowell, M | FLA |
| 43 | Cabrera, O | MON |
| 43 | Vidro, J | MON |
| 42 | Walker, T | CIN |
| 42 | Kent, J | SF |
| 41 | Millar, K | FLA |
| **40** | **Pujols, A** | **STL** |
| 40 | Walker, L | COL |

## Triples

| | | |
|---|---|---|
| 10 | Rollins, J | PHI |
| 8 | Wilkerson, B | MON |
| 8 | Furcal, R | ATL |
| **8** | **Rolen, S** | **STL** |
| 8 | McCracken, Q | ARI |

## Home Runs

| | | |
|---|---|---|
| 49 | Sosa, S | CHI |
| 46 | Bonds, B | SF |
| 42 | Berkman, L | HOU |
| 42 | Green, S | LA |
| 39 | Guerrero, V | MON |
| 38 | Giles, B | PIT |
| 37 | Burrell, P | PHI |
| 37 | Kent, J | SF |
| 35 | Jones, A | ATL |
| **34** | **Pujols, A** | **STL** |

## Runs Batted In

| | | |
|---|---|---|
| 128 | Berkman, L | HOU |
| **127** | **Pujols, A** | **STL** |
| 116 | Burrell, P | PHI |
| 114 | Green, S | LA |
| 111 | Guerrero, V | MON |
| **110** | **Rolen, S** | **STL** |
| 110 | Bonds, B | SF |
| 109 | Helton, T | COL |
| 108 | Kent, J | SF |
| 108 | Sosa, S | CHI |

## Total Bases

| | | |
|---|---|---|
| 364 | Guerrero, V | MON |
| 352 | Kent, J | SF |
| 334 | Berkman, L | HOU |
| **331** | **Pujols, A** | **STL** |
| 330 | Sosa, S | CHI |
| 325 | Green, S | LA |
| 322 | Bonds, B | SF |
| 319 | Burrell, P | PHI |
| 319 | Helton, T | COL |
| 309 | Giles, B | PIT |

## On-Base Percentage

| | | |
|---|---|---|
| .582 | Bonds, B | SF |
| .450 | Giles, B | PIT |
| .435 | Jones, C | ATL |
| .429 | Helton, T | COL |
| .421 | Walker, L | COL |

## On-Base Percentage cont.

| | | |
|---|---|---|
| .420 | **Edmonds, J** | **STL** |
| .417 | Guerrero, V | MON |
| .413 | Abreu, B | PHI |
| .405 | Berkman, L | HOU |
| .404 | Sheffield, G | ATL |

## Slugging Percentage

| | | |
|---|---|---|
| .799 | Bonds, B | SF |
| .622 | Giles, B | PIT |
| .602 | Walker, L | COL |
| .594 | Sosa, S | CHI |
| .593 | Guerrero, V | MON |
| .578 | Berkman, L | HOU |
| .577 | Helton, T | COL |
| .565 | Kent, J | SF |
| **.561** | **Pujols, A** | **STL** |
| **.561** | **Edmonds, J** | **STL** |

## Winning Percentage

| | | | |
|---|---|---|---|
| .828 | Johnson, R | ARI | 24-5 |
| .789 | Miller, W | HOU | 15-4 |
| .767 | Schilling, C | ARI | 23-7 |
| .733 | Stark, D | COL | 11-4 |
| .727 | Nomo, H | LA | 16-6 |
| .727 | Maddux, G | ATL | 16-6 |
| .692 | Millwood, K | ATL | 18-8 |
| **.688** | **Simontacchi, J** | **STL** | **11-5** |
| .679 | Oswalt, R | HOU | 19-9 |

# Team Batting

| Player | AVG | G | AB | R | H | TB | 2B | 3B | HR | RBI | BB | SO | SB | SLG | OBP |
|---|---|---|---|---|---|---|---|---|---|---|---|---|---|---|---|
| Benes, A | .206 | 19 | 34 | 3 | 7 | 11 | 1 | 0 | 1 | 2 | 1 | 9 | 0 | .324 | .229 |
| Cairo, M | .250 | 108 | 184 | 28 | 46 | 65 | 9 | 2 | 2 | 23 | 13 | 36 | 1 | .353 | .307 |
| Coolbaugh, M | .083 | 5 | 12 | 0 | 1 | 1 | 0 | 0 | 0 | 0 | 1 | 3 | 0 | .083 | .154 |
| Crudale, M | .000 | 49 | 2 | 0 | 0 | 0 | 0 | 0 | 0 | 0 | 0 | 1 | 0 | .000 | .000 |
| Cruz, I | .357 | 17 | 14 | 2 | 5 | 8 | 0 | 0 | 1 | 3 | 1 | 3 | 0 | .571 | .400 |
| Delgado, W | .200 | 12 | 20 | 2 | 4 | 12 | 2 | 0 | 2 | 5 | 0 | 6 | 0 | .600 | .200 |
| **RIGHT** | .500 | | 4 | | 2 | 6 | 1 | 0 | 1 | 3 | 0 | 2 | 1 | .500 | .500 |
| **LEFT** | .125 | | 16 | | 2 | 6 | 1 | 0 | 1 | 2 | 0 | 4 | | .375 | .125 |
| DiFelice, M | .230 | 70 | 174 | 17 | 40 | 63 | 11 | 0 | 4 | 19 | 17 | 42 | 0 | .362 | .297 |
| Drew, J | .252 | 135 | 424 | 61 | 107 | 182 | 19 | 1 | 18 | 56 | 57 | 104 | 8 | .429 | .349 |
| Edmonds, J | .311 | 144 | 476 | 96 | 148 | 267 | 31 | 2 | 28 | 83 | 86 | 134 | 4 | .561 | .420 |
| Fassero, J | .333 | 73 | 3 | 0 | 1 | 1 | 0 | 0 | 0 | 0 | 0 | 2 | 0 | .333 | .333 |
| **STL** | .000 | 16 | 0 | 0 | 0 | 0 | 0 | 0 | 0 | 0 | 0 | 0 | 0 | .000 | .000 |
| Finley, C | .107 | 14 | 28 | 2 | 3 | 4 | 1 | 0 | 0 | 1 | 0 | 12 | 0 | .143 | .107 |
| Hackman, L | .063 | 43 | 16 | 0 | 1 | 1 | 0 | 0 | 0 | 0 | 1 | 6 | 0 | .063 | .118 |
| Kile, D | .091 | 14 | 22 | 0 | 2 | 2 | 0 | 0 | 0 | 0 | 1 | 9 | 0 | .091 | .130 |
| Kline, S | .000 | 66 | 1 | 0 | 0 | 0 | 0 | 0 | 0 | 0 | 0 | 0 | 0 | .000 | .000 |
| **RIGHT** | .000 | | 0 | | 0 | 0 | 0 | 0 | 0 | 0 | 0 | 0 | | .000 | .000 |
| **LEFT** | .000 | | 1 | | 0 | 0 | 0 | 0 | 0 | 0 | 0 | 0 | | .000 | .000 |
| Marrero, E | .262 | 131 | 397 | 63 | 104 | 179 | 19 | 1 | 18 | 66 | 40 | 72 | 14 | .451 | .327 |
| Martinez, T | .262 | 150 | 511 | 63 | 134 | 224 | 25 | 1 | 21 | 75 | 58 | 71 | 3 | .438 | .337 |
| Matheny, M | .244 | 110 | 315 | 31 | 77 | 100 | 12 | 1 | 3 | 35 | 32 | 49 | 1 | .317 | .313 |
| Matthews, M | .167 | 47 | 6 | 0 | 1 | 1 | 0 | 0 | 0 | 0 | 0 | 4 | 0 | .167 | .167 |
| **STL** | .167 | 43 | 6 | 0 | 1 | 1 | 0 | 0 | 0 | 0 | 0 | 4 | 0 | .167 | .167 |
| Morris, M | .169 | 32 | 71 | 4 | 12 | 15 | 3 | 0 | 0 | 3 | 3 | 23 | 0 | .211 | .203 |
| Pearce, J | .250 | 3 | 4 | 0 | 1 | 1 | 0 | 0 | 0 | 1 | 0 | 0 | 0 | .250 | .250 |
| Perez, E | .201 | 96 | 154 | 22 | 31 | 70 | 9 | 0 | 10 | 26 | 17 | 36 | 0 | .455 | .290 |
| Polanco, P | .288 | 147 | 548 | 75 | 158 | 221 | 32 | 2 | 9 | 49 | 26 | 41 | 5 | .403 | .330 |
| **STL** | .284 | 94 | 342 | 47 | 97 | 133 | 19 | 1 | 5 | 27 | 12 | 27 | 3 | .389 | .316 |
| Pujols, A | .314 | 157 | 590 | 118 | 185 | 331 | 40 | 2 | 34 | 127 | 72 | 69 | 2 | .561 | .394 |
| Renteria, E | .305 | 152 | 544 | 77 | 166 | 239 | 36 | 2 | 11 | 83 | 49 | 57 | 22 | .439 | .364 |

# Team Batting cont.

| Player | AVG | G | AB | R | H | TB | 2B | 3B | HR | RBI | BB | SO | SB | SLG | OBP |
|---|---|---|---|---|---|---|---|---|---|---|---|---|---|---|---|
| Robinson, K | .260 | 124 | 181 | 27 | 47 | 65 | 7 | 4 | 1 | 15 | 11 | 29 | 7 | .359 | .301 |
| Rodriguez, N | .000 | 2 | 1 | 0 | 0 | 0 | 0 | 0 | 0 | 0 | 0 | 1 | 0 | .000 | .000 |
| Rolen, S | .266 | 155 | 580 | 89 | 154 | 292 | 29 | 8 | 31 | 110 | 72 | 102 | 8 | .503 | .357 |
| STL | .278 | 55 | 205 | 37 | 57 | 115 | 8 | 4 | 14 | 44 | 20 | 34 | 3 | .561 | .354 |
| Simontacchi, J | .240 | 25 | 50 | 5 | 12 | 12 | 0 | 0 | 0 | 2 | 2 | 15 | 0 | .240 | .269 |
| Smith, B | .214 | 11 | 14 | 0 | 3 | 4 | 1 | 0 | 0 | 1 | 1 | 4 | 0 | .286 | .267 |
| Smith, T | .167 | 12 | 18 | 0 | 3 | 3 | 0 | 0 | 0 | 2 | 0 | 6 | 0 | .167 | .167 |
| Stechschulte, G | .000 | 29 | 2 | 0 | 0 | 0 | 0 | 0 | 0 | 0 | 1 | 2 | 0 | .000 | .000 |
| Stephenson, G | .000 | 12 | 12 | 0 | 0 | 0 | 0 | 0 | 0 | 0 | 2 | 8 | 0 | .000 | .077 |
| Taguchi, S | .400 | 19 | 15 | 4 | 6 | 6 | 0 | 0 | 0 | 2 | 2 | 1 | 1 | .400 | .471 |
| Timlin, M | .000 | 72 | 6 | 0 | 0 | 0 | 0 | 0 | 0 | 0 | 0 | 4 | 0 | .000 | .000 |
| STL | .000 | 42 | 6 | 0 | 0 | 0 | 0 | 0 | 0 | 0 | 0 | 4 | 0 | .000 | .000 |
| Veres, D | .333 | 71 | 3 | 0 | 1 | 1 | 0 | 0 | 0 | 0 | 0 | 1 | 0 | .333 | .333 |
| Vina, F | .270 | 150 | 622 | 75 | 168 | 210 | 29 | 5 | 1 | 54 | 44 | 36 | 17 | .338 | .333 |
| White, R | .000 | 61 | 1 | 0 | 0 | 0 | 0 | 0 | 0 | 0 | 0 | 1 | 0 | .000 | .000 |
| STL | .000 | 20 | 1 | 0 | 0 | 0 | 0 | 0 | 0 | 0 | 0 | 1 | 0 | .000 | .000 |
| Williams, W | .207 | 18 | 29 | 3 | 6 | 12 | 3 | 0 | 1 | 3 | 0 | 9 | 0 | .414 | .226 |
| Wright, J | .132 | 23 | 38 | 0 | 5 | 8 | 3 | 0 | 0 | 0 | 0 | 16 | 0 | .211 | .132 |
| STL | .000 | 4 | 5 | 0 | 0 | 0 | 0 | 0 | 0 | 0 | 0 | 3 | 0 | .000 | .000 |
| Pitchers | .160 | 162 | 325 | 17 | 52 | 67 | 9 | 0 | 2 | 15 | 10 | 118 | 0 | .206 | .187 |
| St. Louis | .268 | 162 | 5505 | 787 | 1475 | 2337 | 285 | 26 | 175 | 758 | 542 | 927 | 86 | .425 | .338 |
| Opponents | .251 | 162 | 5402 | 648 | 1355 | 2083 | 275 | 15 | 141 | 621 | 547 | 1009 | 86 | .386 | .323 |

# Team Pitching

| Pitcher | W | L | ERA | G | GS | CG | GF | SHO | SV | IP | H | R | ER | HR | BB | SO |
|---|---|---|---|---|---|---|---|---|---|---|---|---|---|---|---|---|
| Benes, A | 5 | 4 | 2.78 | 18 | 17 | 1 | 0 | 0 | 0 | 97.0 | 80 | 39 | 30 | 10 | 51 | 64 |
| Crudale, M | 3 | 0 | 1.88 | 49 | 1 | 0 | 14 | 0 | 0 | 52.2 | 43 | 11 | 11 | 3 | 14 | 47 |
| Duff, M | 0 | 0 | 4.76 | 7 | 0 | 0 | 1 | 0 | 0 | 5.2 | 3 | 3 | 3 | 0 | 8 | 4 |
| Fassero, J | 8 | 6 | 5.35 | 73 | 0 | 0 | 18 | 0 | 0 | 69.0 | 81 | 43 | 41 | 9 | 27 | 56 |
| STL | 3 | 0 | 3.00 | 16 | 0 | 0 | 1 | 0 | 0 | 18.0 | 16 | 6 | 6 | 4 | 5 | 12 |
| Finley, C | 7 | 4 | 3.80 | 14 | 14 | 1 | 0 | 1 | 0 | 85.1 | 69 | 41 | 36 | 7 | 30 | 83 |
| Hackman, L | 5 | 4 | 4.11 | 43 | 6 | 0 | 9 | 0 | 0 | 81.0 | 90 | 42 | 37 | 7 | 39 | 46 |
| Isringhausen, J | 3 | 2 | 2.48 | 60 | 0 | 0 | 51 | 0 | 32 | 65.1 | 46 | 22 | 18 | 0 | 18 | 68 |
| Joseph, K | 0 | 1 | 4.91 | 11 | 0 | 0 | 6 | 0 | 0 | 11.0 | 16 | 7 | 6 | 1 | 6 | 2 |
| Kile, D | 5 | 4 | 3.72 | 14 | 14 | 0 | 0 | 0 | 0 | 84.2 | 82 | 36 | 35 | 9 | 28 | 50 |
| Kline, S | 2 | 1 | 3.39 | 66 | 0 | 0 | 17 | 0 | 6 | 58.1 | 54 | 23 | 22 | 3 | 21 | 41 |
| Matthews, M | 2 | 1 | 3.94 | 47 | 0 | 0 | 10 | 0 | 0 | 45.2 | 43 | 23 | 20 | 5 | 29 | 34 |
| STL | 2 | 1 | 3.89 | 43 | 0 | 0 | 10 | 0 | 0 | 41.2 | 40 | 21 | 18 | 5 | 22 | 32 |
| Molina, G | 1 | 0 | 1.59 | 12 | 0 | 0 | 3 | 0 | 0 | 11.1 | 6 | 2 | 2 | 1 | 6 | 4 |
| Morris, M | 17 | 9 | 3.42 | 32 | 32 | 1 | 0 | 1 | 0 | 210.1 | 210 | 86 | 80 | 16 | 64 | 171 |
| Pearce, J | 0 | 0 | 7.62 | 3 | 3 | 0 | 0 | 0 | 0 | 13.0 | 20 | 13 | 11 | 1 | 8 | 1 |
| Rodriguez, J | 0 | 0 | 54.00 | 2 | 0 | 0 | 0 | 0 | 0 | 0.1 | 4 | 2 | 2 | 0 | 2 | 0 |
| Rodriguez, N | 0 | 0 | 4.15 | 2 | 0 | 0 | 2 | 0 | 0 | 4.1 | 4 | 3 | 2 | 1 | 1 | 2 |
| Simontacchi, J | 11 | 5 | 4.02 | 24 | 24 | 0 | 0 | 0 | 0 | 143.1 | 134 | 68 | 64 | 18 | 54 | 72 |
| Smith, B | 1 | 5 | 6.94 | 11 | 10 | 0 | 1 | 0 | 0 | 48.0 | 67 | 39 | 37 | 4 | 22 | 22 |
| Smith, T | 4 | 2 | 7.17 | 12 | 10 | 0 | 0 | 0 | 0 | 54.0 | 69 | 44 | 43 | 10 | 20 | 32 |
| Stechschulte, G | 6 | 2 | 4.78 | 29 | 0 | 0 | 5 | 0 | 0 | 32.0 | 27 | 19 | 17 | 4 | 17 | 21 |
| Stephenson, G | 2 | 5 | 5.40 | 12 | 10 | 0 | 0 | 0 | 0 | 45.0 | 48 | 27 | 27 | 4 | 25 | 34 |
| Timlin, M | 4 | 6 | 2.98 | 72 | 1 | 0 | 17 | 0 | 0 | 96.2 | 75 | 35 | 32 | 15 | 14 | 50 |
| STL | 1 | 3 | 2.51 | 42 | 1 | 0 | 10 | 0 | 0 | 61.0 | 48 | 19 | 17 | 9 | 7 | 35 |
| Veres, D | 5 | 8 | 3.48 | 71 | 0 | 0 | 26 | 0 | 4 | 82.2 | 67 | 34 | 32 | 12 | 39 | 68 |
| White, R | 5 | 7 | 4.31 | 61 | 0 | 0 | 10 | 0 | 0 | 62.2 | 62 | 33 | 30 | 4 | 21 | 41 |
| STL | 3 | 1 | 0.82 | 20 | 0 | 0 | 2 | 0 | 0 | 22.0 | 13 | 3 | 2 | 0 | 3 | 14 |
| Williams, W | 9 | 4 | 2.53 | 17 | 17 | 1 | 0 | 0 | 0 | 103.1 | 84 | 30 | 29 | 10 | 25 | 76 |
| Wright, J | 7 | 13 | 5.29 | 23 | 22 | 1 | 0 | 1 | 0 | 129.1 | 130 | 80 | 76 | 17 | 75 | 77 |
| STL | 2 | 0 | 4.80 | 4 | 3 | 0 | 0 | 0 | 0 | 15.0 | 15 | 8 | 8 | 2 | 12 | 8 |
| St. Louis | 97 | 65 | 3.70 | 162 | 162 | 4 | 158 | 2 | 42 | 1446.1 | 1355 | 648 | 595 | 141 | 547 | 1009 |
| Opponents | 65 | 97 | 4.61 | 162 | 162 | 10 | 152 | 10 | 33 | 1433.0 | 1475 | 787 | 734 | 175 | 542 | 927 |

# Transactions

| | |
|---|---|
| 9/27 | Signed 3B S. Rolen to an eight-year contract extension |
| 9/24 | Sent RHP J. Karnuth (New Haven) and RHP J. Blasdell (Peoria) to the Chicago Cubs as the minor-league players to be named in the 8/25 trade for LHP J. Fassero |
| 9/11 | Sent LHP M. Matthews to the Milwaukee Brewers as the player to be named in 8/29 trade for RHP J. Wright |
| 9/7 | Recalled OF S. Taguchi from New Haven (AA) |
| 9/3 | Recalled RHPs J. Simontacchi and G. Molina from Memphis (AAA) |
| | Purchased INF W. Delgado from Memphis |
| | Designated K. McDonald for assignment |
| | Outrighted RHP N. Rodriguez to Memphis |
| 9/2 | Optioned RHP M. Duff to New Haven (AA) |
| 9/1 | Purchased 1B I. Cruz from Memphis (AAA) |
| | Recalled RHP M. Duff from New Haven (AA) |
| 8/30 | Recalled RHP J. Lambert from New Haven (AA) and placed him on the 60-day disabled list |
| | Recalled RHP J. Pearce from Memphis (AAA) and placed him on the 15-day disabled list |
| 8/29 | Optioned RHP J. Simontacchi to Memphis (AAA) |
| | Reinstated RHP W. Williams from the 15-day disabled list |
| | Acquired RHP J. Wright and cash from the Milwaukee Brewers in exchange for minor-league OF C. Morris and a player to be named later |
| 8/28 | Optioned RHP G. Molina to Memphis (AAA) |
| | Reinstated RHP G. Stephenson from the 60-day disabled list |
| | Outrighted RHP K. Joseph |
| 8/26 | Optioned RHP K. Joseph to Memphis (AAA) |
| | Designated RHP D. Nickle for assignment |
| 8/25 | Acquired LHP J. Fassero and cash from the Chicago Cubs in exchange for two minor-league players to be named later |
| 8/24 | Placed RHP M. Morris on the 15-day disabled list (left hamstring) |
| | Placed LHP M. Matthews on the 15-day disabled list (right hip flexor), retroactive to 8/21 |
| | Purchased the contracts of RHP R. White and RHP N. Rodriguez from Memphis (AAA) |
| | Designated INF M. Coolbaugh and OF W. Ortega for assignment |
| 8/17 | Signed free agent RHP R. White and assigned to Memphis (AAA) |
| 8/16 | Outrighted RHP C. Weibl to Memphis (AAA) |
| 8/14 | Optioned RHP M. Duff to Memphis (AAA) |
| | Purchased RHP G. Molina from Memphis (AAA) |
| | Designated RHP C. Weibl for assignment |
| 8/5 | Outrighted RHP T. Smith to Memphis (AAA) |
| 8/1 | Designated RHP T. Smith for assignment |
| | Recalled RHP K. Joseph from Memphis (AAA) |

| 7/30 | Purchased RHP M. Duff from New Haven (AA) |
|---|---|
| 7/29 | Acquired 3B S. Rolen, RHP D. Nickel and cash from the Philadelphia Phillies in exchange for INF P. Polanco, RHP M. Timlin and LHP B. Smith |
| | Assigned RHP D. Nickel to Memphis (AAA) |
| 7/20 | Optioned LHP B. Smith to Memphis (AAA) |
| 7/19 | Acquired LHP C. Finley from the Cleveland Indians in exchange for minor-league OF/1B L. Garcia and a minor-league player to be named later |
| | Signed LHP D. Oliver to a Triple-A contract with Memphis |
| 7/16 | Activated RHP An. Benes from the 60-day disabled list |
| | Optioned INF M. Coolbaugh to Memphis (AAA) |
| | Transferred RHP G. Stephenson from the 15-day disabled list to the 60-day disabled list |
| 7/13 | Activated OF J. Drew from the 15-day disabled list |
| | Placed RHP W. Williams on the 15-day disabled list (left oblique strain), retroactive to 7/7 |
| 7/1 | Optioned RHP G. Stechschulte to Memphis (AAA) |
| | Recalled RHP M. Crudale from Memphis (AAA) |
| 6/30 | Placed OF J. Drew on the 15-day disabled list (right knee tendonitis), retroactive to 6/28 |
| | Purchased INF M. Coolbaugh from Memphis (AAA) |
| 6/27 | Recalled RHP T. Smith from Memphis (AAA) to take the roster spot of the deceased D. Kile |
| 6/16 | Activated OF J. Edmonds from the 15-day disabled list |
| | Optioned OF S. Taguchi to Memphis (AAA) |
| 6/15 | Assigned RHP An. Benes to Memphis (AAA) on a 30-day injury rehabilitation assignment |
| 6/11 | Acquired INF W. Morris from the Minnesota Twins for a player to be named later |
| | Assigned INF W. Morris to Memphis (AAA) |
| | Signed OF G. Williams to a Triple-A contract with Memphis |
| 6/10 | Placed OF J. Edmonds on the 15-day disabled list (sprained right wrist), retroactive to 6/1 |
| | Recalled OF S. Taguchi from Memphis (AAA) |
| 6/5 | Activated LHP R. Ankiel from the 60-day disabled list |
| | Optioned LHP R. Ankiel to Peoria (A) |
| | Outrighted LHP J. Rodriguez to Memphis (AAA) |
| 6/4 | Placed RHP G. Stephenson on the 15-day disabled list (left hamstring strain), retroactive to 5/30 |
| | Recalled LHP B. Smith from Memphis (AAA) |
| 5/31 | Activated LHP S. Kline from the 15-day disabled list |
| | Optioned RHP M. Crudale to Memphis (AAA) |

| 5/29 | Sent LHP S. Kline to New Haven (AA) for injury rehabilitation assignment |
|------|------|
| 5/24 | Sent LHP S. Kline to Peoria (A) for injury rehabilitation assignment |
| 5/15 | Activated RHP W. Williams from the 15-day disabled list |
|      | Optioned B. Smith to Memphis (AAA) |
| 5/7  | Activated RHP G. Stephenson from the 15-day disabled list |
|      | Optioned LHP J. Rodriguez to Memphis (AAA) |
| 5/3  | Optioned RHP J. Pearce to Memphis (AAA) |
|      | Purchased the contract of RHP J. Simontacchi from Memphis |
|      | Transferred RHP A. Benes from the 15-day disabled list to the 60-day disabled list |
| 5/2  | Placed LHP S. Kline (left lat/tricep sprain) on the 15-day disabled list, retroactive to 4/29 |
|      | Purchased the contract of LHP J. Rodriguez from Memphis (AAA) |
|      | Transferred LHP R. Ankiel from the 15-day disabled list to the 60-day disabled list |
| 4/25 | Placed LHP B. Smith (left shoulder strain) on the 15-day disabled list, retroactive to 4/22 |
|      | Recalled RHP G. Stechschulte from Memphis (AAA) |
| 4/18 | Placed RHP A. Benes (right knee) on the 15-day disabled list, retroactive to 4/16 |
|      | Placed RHP G. Stephenson (lower back strain) on the 15-day disabled list, retroactive to 4/15 |
|      | Recalled RHP M. Crudale and RHP J. Pearce from Memphis (AAA) |
| 4/15 | Optioned RHP G. Stechschulte to Memphis (AAA) |
|      | Recalled RHP T. Smith from Memphis |
| 4/11 | Optioned RHP M. Crudale to Memphis (AAA) |
|      | Recalled LHP B. Smith from Memphis |
| 4/6  | Placed RHP W. Williams on the 15-day disabled list (left oblique strain) |
|      | Recalled RHP M. Crudale from Memphis (AAA) |
| 3/30 | Purchased the contract of INF/OF E. Perez from Memphis (AAA) |
|      | Reassigned INF M. Coolbaugh to Memphis |
|      | Optioned LHP B. Smith to Memphis |
| 3/29 | Placed LHP R. Ankiel on the 15-day disabled list (left elbow tendinitis) |
|      | Announced that non-roster OF A. Martin had declined an offer to play at Memphis (AAA) and elected to become a free agent |
| 3/26 | Optioned OF S. Taguchi to Memphis (AAA) |

| 3/24 | Optioned RHP K. Joseph and OF W. Ortega to Memphis (AAA)<br>Traded Memphis OF E. Young to Arizona for a player to be named |
|---|---|
| 3/18 | Optioned RHP J. Pearce to Memphis (AAA)<br>Reassigned OFs T. Mota, L. Saturria and E. Young to the minor-league camp |
| 3/13 | Optioned RHP S. Layfield and C K. McDonald to Memphis (AAA)<br>Reassigned RHPs G. Molina and T. Smith to the minor-league camp |
| 3/12 | Optioned RHPs M. Crudale and J. Lambert to Memphis (AAA)<br>Optioned RHP J. Journell and INF L. Garcia to New Haven (AA)<br>Optioned RHP C. Capel to Potomac (A)<br>Reassigned RHPs K. Sheredy and C. Weibl and INF S. Clapp to the minor-league camp |
| 3/7 | Reassigned INFs R. Balfe, W. Delgado, C. Duncan, C. Haas and C. Snopek and RHP R. Loiselle to the minor-league camp<br>Optioned LHP L. Walrond to New Haven (AA) |
| 3/3 | Reassigned Cs M. Garrick, J. Pogue and B. Waszgis to the minor-league camp |
| 3/2 | Signed 3B A. Pujols to a contract for the 2002 season |
| 3/1 | Signed RHP G. Stechschulte to a contract for the 2002 season |
| 2/26 | Signed LHP M. Matthews to a contract for the 2002 season |
| 2/24 | Signed RHP L. Hackman to a contract for the 2002 season |
| 2/22 | Signed LHP B. Smith to a contract for the 2002 season |
| 2/15 | Opened camp with 38 roster players and 20 non-roster invitees |
| 2/13 | Agreed to contract terms with INF/OF P. Polanco, avoiding salary arbitration |

# Celebrate the Heroes of St. Louis Sports and Mor
## in These Other Acclaimed Titles from Sports Publishing

**Bob Forsch's Tales
from the Cardinals Dugout**
by Bob Forsch and Tom Wheatley
5 1/2 x 8 1/2 hardcover
200 pages
photos throughout
**$19.95**
*2003 release!*

**Jack Buck:
Forever a Winner**
by Carole, Joe, and Julie Buck
8 1/2 x 11 hardcover, 144 pages
color photos throughout
**$24.95**
*2003 release!*

**Ozzie Smith:
The Road to Cooperstown**
by Ozzie Smith with Rob Rains
8 1/2 x 11 hardcover
128 pages
color photos throughout
**$24.95**

**The I-55 Series: Cubs vs.
Cardinals**
by George Castle
and Jim Rygelski
6 x 9 softcover
254 pages
16-page photo section
**$14.95**

**More Tales from the
Red Sox Dugout**
by Bill Nowlin and Jim Prime
5 1/2 x 8 1/4 softcover
200 pages, photos throughout
**$14.95**
*2003 release! Available for the
first time in softcover!*

**More Tales from the
Yankee Dugout**
by Ed Randall
5 1/2 x 8 1/4 softcover, 200 pages
player caricatures throughout
**$14.95**
*2003 release! Available for the
first time in softcover!*

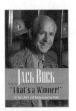

**Jack Buck: "That's a Winner**
by Jack Buck
with Rob Rains and Bob Broeg
6 x 9 softcover
240 pages
16-page photo section
**$14.95**

**Red: A Baseball Life**
by Red Schoendienst
with Rob Rains
6 x 9 hardcover
218 pages
16-page photo section
**$22.95**

**Red: A Baseball Life
(leatherbound edition)**
by Red Schoendienst with Rob Rai
6 x 9 leatherbound, 218 page
16-page photo section
**$99.95**
*All copies signed by Red
Schoendienst, Stan Musial, Lou
Brock, Whitey Herzog, and Rob Ra*

**Eleven Men Believed**
by the *St. Louis Post-Dispatch*
8 1/2 x 11 hardcover and softcove
176 pages
color photos throughout
**$29.95 (hardcover)
$19.95 (softcover)**

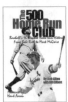

**The 500 Home Run Club**
by Bob Allen with Bill Gilbert
6 x 9 softcover
290 pages
16-page photo section
**$14.95**

**The 3,000 Hit Club**
by Fred McMane
6 x 9 softcover
256 pages
photos throughout
**$14.95**

To order at any time, please call toll-free **877-424-BOOK (2665**
For fast service and quick delivery, order on-line at
## www.SportsPublishingLLC.com.